SALUTE THE KING

George the Sixth and His Far-Flung Realms

BY
ARTHUR MEE

EDITOR OF
THE CHILDREN'S NEWSPAPER

UNIVERSITY OF LONDON PRESS, Ltd.
10 & 11 WARWICK LANE, LONDON, E.C.4
1937
By arrangement with Hodder & Stoughton, Ltd.

Printed in Great Britain for the UNIVERSITY OF LONDON PRESS, LTD., by HAZELL, WATSON AND VINEY LTD. London and Aylesbury.

SALUTE THE KING

GEORGE THE SIXTH

[*Frontispiece*]

THE CHAPTERS

THE PICTURES

THE KING

GEORGE THE SIXTH (Albert Frederick Arthur George) sits in the midst of this changing world on the last great throne in Europe. He is the proud sovereign of one-quarter of the human race, young enough to stand for Youth yet having made himself by his own genius one of the most popular men in his own realm, as by his birth he has become the central figure of the English-speaking world.

He belongs to our Twentieth Century. Nearly all his life has been lived in it, and he has made himself master of its great ideas and its wonderful transformations. He understands its problems, its anxieties, and its opportunities. No King has ever known his own country more intimately, and he has travelled round the world. He has come to the throne not only with the affection of his own people, but with the goodwill of every land. A typical Englishman of his age, he is famous for his universal sympathy and his wide understanding, and everywhere beloved for his naturalness, his frankness, and his simplicity. Following soon upon the most beloved King who ever sat on a throne, he has made it the desire of his life to win for himself the full measure of affection the nation gave to George the Fifth.

He knows the nooks and crannies of our Motherland and many of the great cities and far-off corners of our Empire. He has made himself the friend of all. He has seen the people at work and at play, and the English spirit at its very best runs through him. He has been in our slums and hates them. He has seen war and hates it. He knows our country-side and loves it. He knows the people who are the backbone of our race and has a great sense of brotherhood with them.

He comes to the throne in the prime of manhood. He leads his people at an age when long years loom before him ; he looks into the future and shares our dreams.

It may be that we have never had a king more popular with boys, for George the Sixth was the boy's King most of all when he leapt so suddenly to the throne. He came in a dark hour when his brother had made a bitter choice which almost broke the nation's heart, for Edward the Eighth left his people, his country, and his Empire, and went his way. All too suddenly his younger brother took his place, not with King Edward's long training for twenty-five years as Prince of Wales, not with all his brother's supreme advantages, not with his brother's universal affection and worldwide fame. It was not an easy summons to come like a flash in the night, the summons to give up a quiet life in a happy home with a garden in Piccadilly, and to take upon his shoulders the ceaseless burden of the greatest throne in the world, the widest empire any man has ever ruled.

It was a burden that he could lay down only with his life, and it is known that he did not seek it. Never was it said of him, as it was said of Caesar, that he was ambitious. More perhaps than any of his brothers, he is his father's son, the son of a father beloved throughout the world for a modesty which led him to say in the proudest hour of his life that he could not understand the love of his people, *for he was only a very ordinary sort of fellow*. It is the ambition of George the Sixth to be worthy of the love the nation gave to George the Fifth, and it is because he is like his father that his hundreds of millions of people have rallied round him everywhere.

A king like his father—perhaps, after all, it is ambition, for it is the desire of our country's heart, the thing we would have more than all. It was George the Fifth who cemented the throne and gave it new strength broad-based upon the people's will. He came to it in time of great trouble. He led his people through all the sorrows and bitterness of the Great War. He shared the common sacrifice of all our people, sharing it, it may be said with truth, more deeply than his Parliament. Through the long years of depression that followed the war George the Fifth brought up his sons to believe that the dark days would pass, and led the way in moving the mountain of despair from the path of our people ; and none of his sons was more earnest than he to whom he gave his name and with whom he shared his mind and heart. He has mixed with all kinds of people and been in touch with every sort and grade of life, and always it is the human side of things that appeals to him.

He is a Scout (and the Queen a Guide), and thousands of Scouts know him as a camper. There is no Englishman, no Scotsman, no Welshman, who knows our industries better than he. He has seen men building ships and setting up great buildings, he has been through cotton mills, he has moved freely in every kind of factory, and we may be sure that if he should go down a mine again he would be thrilled to find such a welcome as the miners gave his brother—scrawled in chalk in the eternal darkness of the pit. After George the Fifth and an interval of sorrowful remembrance comes George the Sixth, the king of buoyant youth and hopefulness, an optimist by nature and by wide experience, and it may be said that never has a nation been more happy in such a succession of kings.

He was born at York Cottage on December 14, 1895, and was known as Prince Albert until he was created Duke of York. He played football with the village boys at Sandringham and lived in every way the normal life of an English youth. He went to Osborne and Dartmouth to prepare for the life of a sailor, and when he was eighteen he lived for six months at sea and made his first great journey about the world ; then, coming home again, he became a middy on H.M.S. Collingwood, and there he was a boy of nineteen when the Great War burst upon the world. Even had there been no war it would have been a trying time for him, for in some ways these few years were the decisive years of his life. Twice he was called home for a serious operation, and in the end it was resolved that he was not robust enough for a sailor's life. But not before he had passed through the moving experience of seeing at close quarters the greatest sea battle of all time, for he was at Jutland. He had gone back after his first operation a little too soon in his anxiety to be there, and arrived in time to be present on his ship when the great hour came. He was commended for his coolness and courage during trying hours under fire, and who has not heard the little story of that fateful day told by the officer in command of a gun turret at which the Prince was stationed? When asked what he remembered of it all, the officer could only remember that *the Prince made cocoa for the crew as usual.*

When the time came that he must leave the sea, Prince Albert went to France as captain in the Air Force, and there he was when the Great War ended. Never will he forget the day, for he had the dramatic good fortune to be with King Albert of Belgium when he met his Parliament after four years of exile, sitting with him in the Chamber on November 22, 1918, Prince Albert and King Albert together.

His father had made him a Knight of the Garter, and well worthy he proved himself of this high dignity. Now with his brother Prince Henry he went to Cambridge for a course of history, economics, and civics at Trinity College. While there he was created Duke of York and took his seat in the House of Lords, and, coming home from Cambridge, he was well equipped to take his place as the third gentleman in the land.

All through these years his life was fitting him for the great days looming ahead. He had laid the foundations of his character as his father's son, and more and more the nation saw in him the reflection of his father's virtues. The Navy had called his father the Sprat and his brother the Sardine ; now it called him Johnson. He was always plain Johnson to the officers and Mr Johnson to the men. There is a story of those days which will live now as an example of the British spirit in our kings. Johnson was on the Collingwood as a middy when King

George the Fifth boarded the ship for inspection in the early days of the war. After the inspection the King received the ship's officers on the quarterdeck, and far down on the list according to seniority came Prince Albert. Father and son had not met for months, but the midshipman saluted as Johnson, and the two passed by with not a word of greeting.

Perhaps we should remember the King's great love of fun and play : is he not one of the best of all the friends of the playing-fields ? We recall a story of the months of waiting and watching in the perilous North Sea when a mine or a submarine might at any moment sink a battleship. In our British way it had occurred to those at home to fit out the liner Borodino as a store-ship, and send her north to the Fleet as if she were a floating West End store. Off she went with soles and kippers, honey and jam, shirts and braces, slippers and collar-studs, cigarettes and chocolates, anything a navy might like to buy while waiting. It happened that in the rush hour in this floating store a few middies raided the counter of more than squared with the reckoning, and from behind the counter came a stern rebuke that for the future, while they were in there, these young middies were to keep their hands in their pockets and whistle till they were asked to pay ; then they would not be likely to take anything unauthorised. It was soon after that day that a merry-eyed middy visited the ship and walked into the shop with his hands thrust deep in his pockets and his lips puckered into a whistle, with not a word, but nodding in dumb show with his head to the things he wanted to buy. He was Johnson, King George the Sixth.

It was one of our statesmen who said to a friend,

Watch the Duke of York—he has as sound a judgment as any man I know ; and it was the head of a big works who declared that the Duke had asked the most searching questions ever put to them in the factory. It is known that the King has an immense library on economic and social subjects, but his learning is not all from books. We have had no more practical king on our throne than George the Sixth, who can drive an engine or pilot a plane or make a wireless set. He is a first-class amateur mechanic. He can cast an iron plate, wield a pick, or plant a tree, and for years he had a working bench at his house in Piccadilly. He loves to play a game instead of looking on, to know how to do things rather than to talk about them.

When, on coming home from Cambridge, he looked about for some part to play in public life, he found that the Industrial Welfare Society had been formed, and the Duke became its president. It brought him into touch with men who were doing things, with factories and workshops and mines. He had always believed that a man must find satisfaction in his work and take a pride in the part played in his firm, and this welfare work in industry has enabled him to become familiar at first hand with such questions as the prevention of accidents, the establishment of works councils, pension schemes, thrift schemes, recreations, and health services. He has helped to carry the influence of the Welfare Society all over the land wherever men work with their hands, and it was this interest in factories that gave the Duke an idea which has already affected thousands of lives and will go on influencing thousands more all through our lives.

Welfare work in a factory brought a group of lads

up to London for a fortnight's holiday, and a football
match was arranged for them with the boys of
Westminster School. The Duke kicked off, and as
he sat watching the game the thought came to him
that this mixing of lads was a great idea and should
be followed up. It was done. The first Duke of
York's Camp thus came about. A hundred public
schools and a hundred factories were invited to send
two boys to a holiday camp at New Romney in
Kent. All the boys were from seventeen to nineteen,
and they met for a meal at Buckingham Palace
Mews before they went to camp. They met for a
fortnight, and the Duke went down to them for a
day and a night each week, learning the lesson they
all were learning, *the lesson of living together with those
who share the world with us*.

The Welfare Society's offices are close to Buckingham Palace, near the private business office of the
Duke, and few societies have had a more enthusiastic
or energetic president. It happened one day that
some miners from South Wales called at headquarters,
and the bright idea occurred to someone on the staff
to ring up the president. Soon the door opened and
the Duke was shaking hands with the South Wales
miners, talking over their troubles and giving them a
memory they will not forget. It is this kind of
thing King George likes most of all. He hates sham
ceremony and loves to break out of an official pro-
gramme whenever it can be done. He likes to do
what he wants, to stop and speak to people, to stop a
procession for a moment and look into a cottage that
is not on the list. He is a plain man wanting no
fuss ; he has loved running out to a kinema from his
house in Piccadilly or sitting at home in the evening
doing a cross-word.

And, of course, the King has always loved a game. To hear him laughing at a joke is to think of his father instantly, and he has his father's enjoyment of good sport. He is a first-class man in athletics, the best riding man in his family, a good shot, a polo player a man would be pleased to have on his side ; and, as for tennis, he has played at Wimbledon. He was a good swimmer as a boy of ten. He revels in squash rackets. He is so good a runner that at Cambridge he would do three miles before breakfast. He has the great physical advantage of being completely ambidextrous. He plays tennis left-handed, but polo right-handed. He will play bowls if he is on a bowling-green, but he would rather play billiards. He has always loved the boat race, and long before his college days he and his brother had frightened Buckingham Palace and alarmed the police by slipping out on the Saturday morning, making their way through the crowds, and arriving quietly on the police-boat while hundreds of police were seeking them. He learned cricket from W. G. Grace, champion of champions, the marvellous man who in 43 years made 126 centuries, scoring 54,896 runs and taking 2876 wickets. It was such a king of cricket who taught our King our national game, and well he learned his lesson, for the day came when Prince Albert was to accomplish a hat trick without parallel. He was playing at Windsor, and with three balls he bowled the King his father, the Prince of Wales his brother, and his cousin Arthur of Connaught.

W. G. Grace for cricket and Richard Kearton for Nature—truly the King has learned from great teachers. It was a lantern lecture given on his birthday by Mr Kearton which gave Prince Albert a close insight into the wonders of Nature about us, and Mr Kearton long remembered how, at the end of the lecture, the Prince came up to ask questions for himself and a few for his young brother, saying, " You know, my brother is shy ; he does not like to talk to strangers."

King George is a good scout. If we rang up his house in Piccadilly, it was a scout who answered the telephone. If we called at his business office in Grosvenor Crescent, it was a scout in bright uniform who opened the door. Out of his scouts grew his great love of playing-fields. He is President of the Playing Fields Association, and no man has done more to find room for play in England's green and pleasant land.

And far away our King has been in the lands of the flag ; long before he came to the throne he had seen something of life on four continents. While he was still in his teens he went out to the West Indies and saw the great port of Halifax in Nova Scotia, saw the great city of Quebec where French and British live in perfect harmony side by side, saw our oldest colony of Newfoundland, the marvellous Falls of Niagara, and the cities of Ottawa and Montreal.

Before his next long tour, a splendid Empire journey which took him round the world, the Duke had married, finding a wife in Scotland to his people's great delight. The bride was Lady Elizabeth Bowes-Lyon, the Earl of Strathmore's daughter, and her home was the famous Glamis Castle, the home of Macbeth. It comes into Shakespeare as a very pleasant seat where the air is delicate, and where the temple-haunting martlet loves to be. Here in Scotland and in the pleasant English country of Hertfordshire Lady Elizabeth grew up with her brothers, and she had the poignant experience of seeing all her brothers go to the war, one of them not coming back. She was only fourteen when the war broke out, having been born in the last summer of last century, and she had lived an outdoor life, running a Girl Guide troop at Glamis and sharing in all the recreations of the countryside. Young though she was, the Great War was real to her, for she saw the old castle become a hostel for wounded, and she grew up to womanhood in the shadow of the affliction that fell upon the world. She is a thorough democrat, a good housewife who can make cakes and scones with any Scottish farmer's wife, is good at languages, a gifted musician, rides fearlessly and well, and delights in games.

It is not surprising that her engagement to Prince Albert, the union of a king's son with a commoner, stirred honest enthusiasm among the people. The King announced it " with great pleasure " and it was a lovely wedding. The public raised a fund of £25,000 for the royal couple, which they spent in giving treats and holidays for workers in industrial areas. The marriage took place in Westminster Abbey, and one thing that happened will never be forgotten by thousands of people, for as the bride walked from the altar through the abbey's stately nave she stopped just beyond the grave of David Livingstone and laid her flowers on the Unknown Warrior's grave. There have been brides who have bequeathed their jewels for the cross on the altar, and wives who gave their wedding rings for hanging the Lenten veil in Westminster Cathedral ; it was a sublime impulse akin to these that moved our Scottish princess to pay this beautiful tribute in her happiest hour to those who gave their lives for us.

The Duke was already famous for his interest in men and boys, and the Duchess was soon to be famous for her work among women and girls. She has won universal admiration, and it is true that never was a royal choice or a royal bride more welcomed by a people, and never did a princess better deserve the popularity she has won. The birth of two princesses brought a new joy into our royal house, and the nation has watched with much interest the delightful ways of Princess Elizabeth and Princess Margaret Rose.

It is believed in some quarters that the presence of two sisters next to the throne may raise a difficult question for the British Constitution, for it would appear, according to some authorities, that by the Law of Succession both sisters have an equal claim to the throne. It is a situation the British Constitution had not clearly foreseen, and the matter has now engaged the careful attention of Parliament. What is certain is that never were two sisters more popular than these, Elizabeth born on April 21, 1926, and Margaret Rose born on August 21, 1930. They have been brought up in great simplicity, and countless stories have been told which have endeared them to all hearts. In Scotland Margaret Rose is beloved because she was born at Glamis (born in that castle of strange tales on a wild and stormy night), the only heir to the throne born in Scotland since Charles the First. Princess Elizabeth (we are told that she would take up the telephone when quite a little child and say, *Mummie, come to Lillibeth*) has a dignity in public consistent with the natural frankness of an English girl, and it was lovely to see her leading Margaret Rose in waving to the people at George the Fifth's Silver Jubilee.

It is the happy home life of our King and Queen that has won for them the grateful loyalty of the nation. It is the secret of the strength of the British people that it has always had a deep and vigorous faith in the importance of the home and in the domestic virtues which spring from a happy fireside, and in the days of George the Sixth, as in the days of George the Fifth, the throne is cemented by the affection of father, mother, and children, the domestic scene beloved throughout the English-speaking world.

The Duke and Duchess early in their married life gave themselves the wonderful experience of seeing Africa. They saw the primitive country and the ancient peoples, and travelled at times, not like king's sons and royal daughters, but like the pioneer making his way through rough country. These first great memories they stored up together will live long with them.

They saw Somalis and Arabs and Negroes run wild with enthusiasm. They saw extraordinary native dances and scenes of frenzied excitement in native settlements. They saw the quaint life of the bazaars and little towns surrounded by coconut plantations. They sat in front of the engine watching wild beasts scuttle away to the jungle and run across the rails. They spent a Christmas morning in the English church in Nairobi with two thousand natives round them and Kiswahili prayer-books in their hands. They made their way through gloomy forest and trackless wilderness, and saw their cars waterlogged. They saw the lion and the rhinoceros cross their path ; the Duke fired at one so that it ran into the bush, driving out two angry buffaloes.

In Uganda they found a young king who speaks English, the Kabaka of the Buganda, aged 29, a charming young man who was knighted by the Duke while his Parliament knelt about him to give thanks, and the warriors came following with their wild cries. They rode two hundred miles to see the Lukiko of Fort Portal at work, the parliament of a native town, and found vast crouching crowds of natives beating tomtoms and playing on reeds to make known the virtues of the king's son and his wife. They went into the Semliki Valley, where Solomon collected ivory for the Queen of Sheba, but where the only drinking-water was deep brown stuff well filled with mud which must be strained with alum, and where live forest pigs and chimpanzees, gorillas, zebras, and the hippopotamus. They left their steamer where the White Nile roars and falls and tosses for a hundred miles, and went by car, camping on the way ; the Duchess is an admirable camper (for is she not a Guide ?) and little did she mind when the storm blew her tent down in the night. They were living the life of wild Africa, Africa as it was before the light came to the Dark Continent. Once they saw 12,000 Nubian warriors dance and wrestle and hurl their spears.

But it was not all primitive life on this African tour, for they saw something of the marvellous transformation that has come about—the great Sennar Dam which was then being finished and was to irrigate parched lands and bring new life into the desert. They saw Khartoum, passing through triumphal arches on the spot where Gordon died, and they came through the Suez Canal in a blinding storm.

Home again from this surprising journey the Duke and Duchess settled down, Princess Elizabeth was

born, and in six months they were off again, this time
to the ends of the earth. Here already our future
king was following in his father's steps, for George the
Fifth had opened the Commonwealth Parliament of
Australia at the dawn of the twentieth century, and
the son who was to be George the Sixth was now to
open the Parliament House in Australia's new capital
of Canberra. It was an interesting journey there.
They sighted Teneriffe and the guns boomed out to
greet the friendly land of Spain. They had a little
time with the people of Jamaica, and we remember
that at Kingston the Duke made himself popular
by letting them see how he hated fuss, for the mayor
had forgotten the key of the casket containing an
address and the Duke put right his embarrassment by
taking the locked casket with a smile : such a good
mechanic as he would know well how to open it !

In the Panama Canal they saw the huge gates
opened for them and the rushing waters leap into a
mountain of foam on their way to the Atlantic.
In the South Seas their good ship Renown called at
the little bay of Nukuhiva, where the wall of rock rises
a thousand feet high with steep green slopes and a
lovely village peeps out from palms and banana trees.
The natives were greatly excited, and the French
Administrator came to greet the royal travellers in a
whaler rowed by six Polynesians with coronets of
flowers. At Fiji the natives prepared strange mix-
tures from roots, poured them into an ancient
battered bowl, strained it to remove the grit, and
offered it to the Duke ; and for the Duchess they
presented whale's teeth, so precious that in the days
before the Flag came here each one of them would
buy two wives. In New Zealand the loyalty of the
people knew no bounds, and children travelled

eighty miles over rough ground to greet the King's
son.   He drove the train through the longest tunnel
in the island.   In Tasmania they rode under four
triumphal arches, one of wool, one of fruit, one of
minerals, and one representing the electric power that
is working such modern wonders in this ancient land.
In Melbourne a procession of war veterans passed
by with the Duke at the salute, and there were thirty
winners of the Victoria Cross among them.   At
Adelaide two little children came up to the platform
and gave them two threepenny bits for Baby's
money box.

They saw the great city and the great harbour of
Sydney in the days before our English engineers had
thrown the steel bridge across the waters.   They
brought back from the women of Victoria the Toc H
banner of their State, so that they might set it in the
Toc H Church of All Hallows by-the-Tower.   They
saw the life of Australia in the teeming centres of its
population and in the backlands.   They came across
Blackfellows in Australia and Maoris in New Zealand,
and heard with great delight that both these ancient
races remembered their royal forerunners.

They met an old Dane of 88, a pioneer farmer of
Australia, who stirred the emotion of the Duke and
Duchess by telling them that he had been in the guard
of honour to Princess Alexandra when she left
Denmark for her English marriage.

But their chief experience was, of course, the event
which had brought them across the world, the
opening of the new Parliament House of Australia
in the new capital of the continent.   It is the only
Parliament in the world that rules an entire continent,
and the city of Canberra has been laid out, 200 miles

from Sydney and 300 miles from Melbourne, as the official capital of the Australian people. On a grave not far from the centre of the capital is a stone with the words : *For here we have no abiding city, but we seek one to come.* The woman who sleeps in the grave died when Canberra was a sheep run. Today there has grown up about her a city abiding indeed, for it rules the vast island continent and is bound to grow as the development of the Twentieth Century brings millions of people to the spacious farmlands and the magnificent cities of the Commonwealth. There were men present in the Parliament House who remembered Canberra before a stone of the capital had been laid, and it was a thrilling day for them when King George's son George declared the Commonwealth Parliament open in its new home. This is what the King's son said to them :

Today marks the end of one epoch and the beginning of another, and one's thoughts turn instinctively to what the future may have in store. Life would hardly be worth living without its dreams of better things, and the life of a nation without such dreams of a better and larger future would be poor indeed.

Standing and looking out over the beautiful site chosen for your Federal capital, I think of those great men who worked for a federated Australia. We are building on the foundations they laid.

I think we should all have in our hearts one other vision. On Anzac Day we commemorated those gallant men and women who laid down their lives in the war. Though they have passed into the Great Beyond they are still speaking to those who choose to listen ; and if Australia listens to the voices of that noble army of dead, and if the great army of those living and those yet unborn is determined to march in step with them toward the ideals for which they died, then a glorious destiny for this country will be assured.

How much has happened in the quarter of a century since the opening of the first Commonwealth Parliament! What changes in the world, what a revolution in human life and thought, what marvellous progress in means of communication and loco-motion! For Australia and the whole Empire it has been a period of extraordinary evolution and development. It has been a testing time, when under the stress of the greatest war in history the Empire has found a new meaning and a new strength.

Quickened by all these influences without and within, the British Empire has advanced to a new conception of harmony and freedom, to the idea of a system of British Nations, each freely ordering its own individual life.

As they left the Continent a plaintive Coo-ee came from the people on the shore and the band of the Renown played Auld Lang Syne. On their way home they were impressed with the twin peaks of Mauritius dominating the island from their height of half a mile above the sea, and they were given a map of the island in silver, with its roads and rail-ways in silver threads, rubies for lighthouses, a sapphire for Port Louis, and diamonds for the factories where the sugar comes from. We may be sure the travellers were sorry they could stay but two days in this wonderful island, although the local paper, meaning to tell the people that the Duke and Duchess could not stay more than two days, made a slip and told them that the Duke and Duchess could not *stand* more than two days in Mauritius!

At Malta the travellers had a fine reception, and at Gibraltar they went to see the famous Water-works which are one of the wonders of the island. There is very little rain in summer on Gibraltar, though throughout the year the average fall is more than England's. As there is no other source of drinking-water the rain is precious and must be carefully preserved. Collecting areas have been constructed high up on the rock, and one of the most striking features to be seen as we approach Gibraltar from the east is the shining face of a slope of rock from which the water drains down. The collecting areas cover sixteen acres, and the vast underground tanks hold over six million gallons. The Renown reached home in the summer of 1927, the Duke's three brothers meeting him at Spithead. He was back with a knowledge of the Empire that was to be of great value to him when, as the most serious of all his father's sons, his turn came to take his place at the head of them all.

At home, as in the Empire, it was a busy life that lay before the Duke, but first of all there was the deep manifestation of affection which greeted the parents at Buckingham Palace as they stepped on to the balcony after their arrival at Victoria. This time the Duchess had her Elizabeth in her arms, already beginning to be a little Princess Charming, and the mother who had yearned for her so long held her up to the assembled people with a pride that was only equalled by their joy.

After this—Home. There was to be no splendid palace for these simple people ; 17 Bruton Street and 145 Piccadilly were good enough for them until they reached the Throne itself. Very soon they were back to the busy life of those who love their country. There was a speech at the Guildhall, in which the Duke declared that he had come home a thorough optimist, believing that we were bound to win through the Depression if we held together. There were many trees planted, a joyful thing to do which both of them love, and which they have done with delight in many countries on three continents. There was a visit to Glasgow to see the Corporation Housing Plan at work, and an endless round of duties which were crowned in the autumn of that year by a day which the Duke counted one of the happiest and most important of his life.

It was a romantic day in the history of Scotland when the Duke was appointed High Commissioner to the General Assembly of the Church of Scotland, for it was the red-letter Assembly of 1929, when the Old Church and the United Free Church came together again after a separation of more than eighty years. The Duke attended the Assembly at Holyrood Palace on behalf of the King, and it was a moving occasion when the last act took place, and the Moderators of Auld Kirk and Free Kirk shook hands with much solemnity on the deed that made the Churches one ; they were in a huge omnibus garage with twelve thousand people looking on, and in that vast company was a lady of Perth who had been present as a child at the Separation nearly ninety years before.

It was a great delight to Scotland when the Duke shared this historic event with them, and it was a greater delight still when, in the following summer, Princess Margaret Rose was born at Glamis.

In a hundred other ways the Duke endeared himself to Youth, by associating himself with their movements, and especially by encouraging among them the healthy outdoor life. When he came to the Throne as King there were throughout the country more than six thousand boys from factories and public schools who had mixed together in their pleasures and learned to understand each other by

life in the Duke of York's Camp. Scouts and Boy
Brigaders loved the Prince who shared their life with
them. He was at the Jubilee of the Boys' Brigade
in the Albert Hall in the summer of 1935, and received a silver baton carried by three thousand boys
in relays, running day and night for a distance of
2309 miles. He made a great tour of the Midlands,
and visited Tyneside, and went down a pit, and when
his father died he took over many of his brother's
activities to relieve the pressure on the new King.
One splendid piece of work he crowned by his great
interest in it—the building up of Middlesex Hospital
which for so many years was falling down. He had
laid the foundation stone seven years before, and in
1935 he opened the new building and was cheered
by receiving two gifts of fifty thousand pounds.

And in all his public and private work it was
noticed increasingly that the thing that came upper-
most in the character of the Duke was his naturalness
and frankness. He was plainly honest in all that he
did, hating pretence. We must believe that he
meant what he said when a man came up to him at a
wayside station in Tasmania and said, "I have come
all the way from Hobart to see you," and the Duke
replied, "And I have come all the way from England
to see you." Coming home through the Suez Canal,
he saw British troops cheering wildly on the shore
and recognised among them the Somerset Light
Infantry, of which he is Colonel-in-Chief. Almost
before they knew it the Duke was ashore to inspect
his regiment. Such a man he is ; so close to our
lives does he wish to be.

The more his people see of him the more they know
that every day our George the Sixth is becoming
every inch a King. Those who remember the thrill

of emotion surging through the world when the life
of King George passed peacefully to its close will
remember also the pathetic scene when our King and
his brothers walked for miles bareheaded through
London, along the streets through which they rode
in triumph at King George's jubilee. They will not
forget that scene, so proud, so poignant, when at a
late hour at night the King and his brothers walked
quietly into Westminster Hall to guard their father's
coffin for half an hour while the mourning throng
passed by. It was the sad beginning of a new reign
and a new era, and none who saw him can forget the
sorrowful figure of the King. He stood in that hour
of sorrow as the symbol of Grief for all of us ; today
he stands as the symbol of Hope. He knows his
people intimately. He knows their trials and problems, and the things they delight in.

In front of him lie the years in which peace or war
are in the balance for mankind, and before him is the
vision of civilisation itself in the scales. They are
years of grave anxiety and dazzling opportunity, of
anxiety whether the nations will let the universal
peace slip from them, of the opportunity to lift up
men's hearts and set them free from fear. Whatever
destiny may come, we have a ruler who will share the
future with us, serving us as he has served us in the
past, with loyalty and selflessness. We feel that
from being a sort of quiet brother to the people, he
will become our Captain and our King.

THE CROWN

TWO crowns has King George, a crown that is called Content, the universal affection of his people, and the jewelled crown with which he is invested in the Abbey, the greatest burden borne by any man.

It is the personal symbol of the highest office any man can hold in this world, for it invests him with the solemn lordship of one quarter of the human race. This crown of a thousand years, glittering with gems, stands for the rise of the English-speaking peoples from a small nation to a mighty Empire. It takes us back to the days before the Conqueror came, to the King who started Westminster Abbey, and from then till now the crown has been the symbol of power for kings and people in these British Isles and in our far dominions through the world.

Now the old crown opens a new chapter. Something has happened to it that has made it six crowns in one. Whatever may have been its glory in the past, it is today the most impressive jewel on the earth, for it is the only visible link that binds the British Empire into one.

A solemn change has come about since George the Fifth was crowned, and no more does the Coronation Service of his ancestors make a man King of the Empire and Emperor of India. For the first time in history the King must be crowned imperially, in the presence of the representatives of the Dominions.

Daughter States no more, they are Sisters with the Motherland, and the kings of our time have been the first of all our kings to rule over dominions beyond the government of our own Parliament.

This glittering crown that binds five hundred million people into one—what is it ?

The Imperial State Crown (worn by the King not at his actual crowning but at all great State occasions afterwards) begins with a velvet cap with an ermine border, lined with white silk ; it becomes a circlet enriched with thousands of precious stones, surmounted with a ball and a cross.   In the middle of the cross is a sapphire from a ring worn by Edward the Confessor on his finger, worn by him, we need not doubt, as he sat thinking he would build an Abbey at Westminster.   In the base of the crown is a great ruby from the helmet of the Black Prince, and between the sapphire and the ruby are two pearl ear-rings worn by Queen Elizabeth.   It is something to thrill us as we think of it, for this sapphire from the Confessor's ring (buried with him in his coffin by King Harold, it is said) comes from the days when it was supposed to have miraculous powers.   This ruby was with the Black Prince on all his battlefields, at Crécy and Poitiers, and was worn by Henry the Fifth at Agincourt, just missed, it is believed, by a sword-thrust on his helmet.   These pearls were worn by Queen Elizabeth in the dazzling pageantry of our Golden Age.   We feel that there is something more than we can see in this majestic diadem.

True it is that there is more than we can see in this great crowning.   It comes out of a primitive past into the age of wonder that we live in.   We must think it fitting that the King will be crowned sitting on a stone kept sacred for a thousand years, the Stone of Scone with legends going back to Jacob and history going back to Alfred. There has grown up about it a marvellous coronation pageantry, but all the pomp and ceremonial, all the regalia and all the wonder of this famous spectacle, stand for things unseen. They stand for the idea the people have of the King; they are the symbol of the spirit of kingship as our people have understood it down the ages.

It is true that a nation can live without a king, but it was something in the early days for men to rally round a chief, and it is easy, when we think of the scattered peasants and the warring tribes of Saxon England, to understand what Alfred meant to them. It is easy to understand what the Conqueror meant when he came with his Normans to shape this country into a nation. It is not easy to think of our great Tudor Age without the stately figure of Elizabeth receiving the Spanish Ambassador, knighting Sir Francis Drake, moving in procession among her people. Great sovereigns are like a magnet, drawing their peoples to them and binding them as one.

So it is that when the Archbishop of Canterbury, and the Lord Chancellor, and all the ceremonial officers of state present King George to his people in the Abbey (amid the acclamation of the spectators, with the boys of Westminster School among them), they are presenting to the nation the leader we have chosen to stand for us before the world. It is not for nothing, all this stately ceremony; it is our way of clothing the King with solemn power and high authority, of saying to him the great things we expect of him, of reminding ourselves and declaring to the world what our crowned King stands for.

It is a long and mysterious ceremonial at which the King is invested with the Crown.   The rich regalia is laid on the altar, and after a short sermon the Archbishop of Canterbury puts to the King the Coronation Oath.   This is what the King swears to do :

To govern the people of his realms according to the statutes of Parliament and their laws and customs ;

To cause law and justice in mercy to be done in all judgments to the utmost of his power ;

To maintain and obey the laws of God, to be faithful to the Gospel, and to maintain the Protestant religion ;

To maintain and preserve inviolable the doctrine and worship and discipline of the Church of England.

The long series of ceremonies that now takes place before the crowning, and those that follow on the crowning, are all intended to impress the King and the people with the deep solemnity of the event.   It is intended that the King should be clothed in sanctity and purity and justice.   He is anointed, robed in proud vestments, and invested with symbols of power and justice and mercy.   With the Sword of State carried before him, the King goes to the altar and makes his solemn oath before the people, his right hand on the Bible as he says : *The things which I have herein promised I will perform and keep.   So help me God*.   The King then returns to the chair for the Anointing.   The gold vessel with the consecrated oil for anointing the King (the Ampulla) is like a golden eagle, and the oil comes from the beak ; it is believed that it was used at the coronation of Henry the Fourth in 1399.

Before the anointing a hymn is sung, the Archbishop offers a prayer that the King shall receive the spirit

of wisdom and government, of counsel and knowledge and godliness, and that he shall be filled with the fear of God for ever ; and then the King takes off his Cap of State, goes to the altar, sits in his chair, and is anointed. Four knights hold over him a rich pall of silk or cloth of gold, and the Dean of Westminster, taking the ampulla and spoon from the altar, fills the spoon with oil. The Primate dips his finger into it, and with it touches the King on the breast, the crown of the head, and the palms of his hands. The Primate then offers a prayer that the work of his hands may prosper :

That by heavenly grace you may preserve the people committed to your charge in wealth, peace, and godliness ; and after a long and glorious course of ruling this temporal kingdom wisely, justly, and religiously, you may at last be made partaker of an eternal kingdom.

Now the Dean puts on the King a sleeveless robe of soft fine linen edged with lace, with a thick gold cord, and over it a mantle of cloth of gold. He is then presented with spurs, richly wrought in gold, as symbols of chivalry ; an officer touches his heels with them and the spurs are then returned to the altar. Now the Lord Chancellor lays a sword on the altar as a symbol of justice, the Archbishop offering a prayer that the King may not use it in vain, but as the minister of God for the terror and punishment of evildoers and the protection and encouragement of those who do well. The Lord Chamberlain girds the King with the sword and the Primate then says to the King :

With this Sword do justice, stop the growth of iniquity, protect the Holy Church of God, help and

THE KING LEAVES BUCKINGHAM PALACE

*defend widows and orphans, restore the things that are
gone to decay, maintain the things that are restored,
punish and reform what is amiss, and confirm what is
in good order ; that doing these things you may be
glorious in all virtue, and so faithfully serve our Lord
Jesus Christ in this life that you may reign for ever
with him in the life which is to come.*

The King takes off the sword and lays it on the
altar in its scabbard, returning to his chair, where-
upon a peer, having redeemed the sword, draws it
from the scabbard and bears it naked before the
King during the rest of the service.

Now the King is invested with the Armilla (a band
worn over the shoulders) and the imperial mantle,
and there is then brought to him the Orb, a globe of
gold round which run bands of diamonds, rubies,
emeralds, sapphires, and pearls, an amethyst at the
top bearing a jewelled cross. The Orb is meant to
remind the sovereign and to declare to the people
that all the powers of kings and all the kingdoms of
this world are subject to the empire of Christ.

As the Primate delivers the Orb into the King's
hands he says :

*Receive this Imperial Robe and Orb ; and the Lord
your God endue you with knowledge and wisdom, with
majesty and with power from on high. The Lord
clothe you with the Robe of Righteousness, and with
the garments of salvation. And when you see this
Orb set under the Cross, remember that the whole world
is subject to the power and Empire of Christ our
Redeemer.*

The King now gives the Orb for the Dean to
return to the altar, and an officer of the Jewel House
delivers the King's ring, which the Primate puts on

the fourth finger of King George as a sign of kingly dignity, saying :

Receive this Ring, the ensign of kingly dignity, and of Defence of the Catholic Faith ; and as you are this day solemnly invested in the government of this earthly kingdom, so may you be sealed with that Spirit of promise which is the earnest of a heavenly inheritance, and reign with Him who is the blessed and only Potentate, to whom be glory for ever and ever. Amen.

The King then receives in his right hand the Sceptre with the Cross as the emblem of kingly power and justice, and in his left hand the Sceptre with the Dove as the symbol of righteousness and mercy, the Archbishop saying :

Receive the Rod of Equity and Mercy: and God, from whom all holy desires, all good counsels, and all just works do proceed, direct and assist you in the administration and exercise of all those powers which He hath given you. Be so merciful that you be not too remiss ; so execute justice that you forget not mercy. Punish the wicked, protect and cherish the just, and lead your people in the way wherein they should go.

Now, standing by the altar, the Archbishop takes up the crown and offers this prayer :

O God, the Crown of the faithful, Bless we beseech thee and sanctify this thy servant George our King ; and, as thou dost this day set a crown of pure gold upon his head, so enrich his royal heart with thine abundant grace, and crown him with all princely virtues.

The King returns to the Coronation chair, and the crown is brought from the altar by the Dean and set on the King's head by the Primate. At the sight of this the people crowding the Abbey cry with loud and repeated shouts, *God Save the King*, the peers put on their coronets, the trumpets sound, and the great guns are fired at the Tower. The acclamation ceasing, the Primate says to the crowned King :

Be strong and of a good courage. Observe the commandments of God, and walk in His holy ways. Fight the good fight of faith and lay hold on eternal life, that in this world you may be crowned with success and honour, and when you have finished your course receive a crown of righteousness, which God the righteous Judge shall give you in that day.

The choir then sings :

Be strong and play the man. Keep the commandments of the Lord thy God and walk in His ways.

The Dean now presents the King with the Bible from the altar, saying :

Our Gracious King, we present you with this Book, the most valuable thing that this world affords. Here is Wisdom : this is the Royal Law ; these are the lively Oracles of God.

After the singing of Te Deum the King is led to his throne by the bishops and peers, and on the throne receives homage—first from the Primate who has crowned him and now pays homage with the bishops, then from the royal princes, then from the senior peers of the five ranks of the peerage : a duke, a marquis, an earl, a viscount, and a baron. All who pay homage touch the crown and kiss the King on the cheek.

With the nobles who have borne the regalia gathered round the steps of the throne, the Coronation ends, the Primate saying these words before the King departs :

Stand firm, and hold fast from henceforth the seat and state of royal and imperial dignity, which is this day delivered unto you in the name and by the authority of Almighty God, and by the hands of us the bishops and servants of God, though unworthy ; and, as you see us to approach nearer to God's Altar, so vouchsafe the more graciously to continue to us your royal favour and protection.

And the Lord God Almighty, whose ministers we are, and the stewards of His mysteries, establish your throne in righteousness, that it may stand fast for evermore, like as the sun before him and as the faithful witness in heaven. Amen.

Who can imagine the solemn feeling of a King in these hours of his crowning ? The thought came to Shakespeare, and comes into a famous scene. Henry the Fourth lay dying, his conscience uneasy, his physical frame in the grip of disease, and the Prince of Wales was by his bed, alone, when the King fell into a deathlike trance, and it seemed to his son that the crown had fallen to his lot.

All the world knows the stories of the youth of the Prince of Wales who was to become the hero king of Agincourt. There is no truth in half of them, but true it is that his youth was wild and that his life was changed as by a miracle when the kingship came to him. If we take Shakespeare's view, it was the crown that brought the change. Sitting watching by the King the Prince is made to say :

> Why doth the crown lie there upon his pillow,
> Being so troublesome a bedfellow ?
> O polished perturbation, golden care,
> That keep'st the ports of slumber open wide
> To many a watchful night, sleep with it now !

Then, thinking that the King is not to wake again,
the Prince of Wales takes up the crown (the rigol, as
Shakespeare calls it, meaning a circle) :

My gracious lord ! my father !
This sleep is sound indeed ; this is a sleep
That from this golden rigol hath divorced
So many English kings.   Thy due from me
Is tears and heavy sorrows of the blood,
Which nature, love, and filial tenderness,
Shall, O dear father, pay thee plenteously !
My due from thee is this imperial crown,
Which, as immediate from thy place and blood,
Derives itself to me.   Lo, here it sits,
Which heaven shall guard ! and, put the world's whole
    strength
Into one giant arm, it shall not force
This lineal honour from me ! this from thee
Will I to mine leave, as tis left to me.

Suddenly the King wakes, and his dying heart
is broken as he feels that his wild son has seized
the crown so soon :

Dost thou so hunger for mine empty chair
That thou wilt needs invest thee with my honours
Before thy hour be ripe ?   O foolish youth !
Thou seek'st the greatness that will overwhelm thee.
Stay but a little ; for my cloud of dignity
Is held from falling with so weak a wind
That it will quickly drop ! my day is dim.
Thou hast stolen that which after some few hours
Were thine without offence ; and at my death
Thou hast sealed up my expectation.
Thy life did manifest thou lovedst me not,
And thou wilt have me die assured of it.
Thou hid'st a thousand daggers in thy thoughts,
Which thou hast whetted on thy stony heart
To stab at half an hour of my life.

What ! canst thou not forbear me half an hour ?
Then get thee gone and dig my grave thyself,
And bid the merry bells ring to thine ear
That thou art crownèd, not that I am dead.
Let all the tears that should bedew my hearse
Be drops of balm to sanctify thy head.
Only compound me with forgotten dust ;
Give that which gave thee life unto the worms.
Pluck down my officers, break my decrees ;
For now a time is come to mock at form !
Henry the Fifth is crowned ! up, vanity !
Down, royal state ! all you sage counsellors, hence !
And to the English court assemble now,
From every region, apes of idleness.
O my poor kingdom, sick with civil blows !
When that my care could not withhold thy riots,
What wilt thou do when riot is thy care ?
O, thou wilt be a wilderness again,
Peopled with wolves, thy old inhabitants !

Now it is the Prince whose heart is breaking : till
now he could not speak for tears :

O, pardon me, my liege ! but for my tears,
The moist impediments unto my speech,
I had forestalled this dear and deep rebuke
Ere you with grief had spoke and I had heard
The course of it so far.   There is your crown ;
And He that wears the crown immortally
Long guard it yours !
God witness with me, when I here came in,
And found no course of breath within your majesty,
How cold it struck my heart !   If I do feign,
O, let me in my present wildness die
And never live to show the incredulous world
The noble change that I have purposèd !
Coming to look on you, thinking you dead,
(And dead almost, my liege, to think you were),
I spake unto this crown as having sense,

And thus upbraided it : *The care on thee depending*
Hath fed upon the body of my father ;
Therefore, thou best of gold art worst of gold :
Other, less fine in carat, is more precious,
Preserving life in medicine potable ;
But thou, most fine, most honoured, most renowned,
Hast eat thy bearer up. Thus, my most royal liege,
Accusing it, I put it on my head,
To try with it, as with an enemy
That had before my face murdered my father,
The quarrel of a true inheritor.
But if it did infect my blood with joy,
Or swell my thoughts to any strain of pride ;
If any rebel or vain spirit of mine
Did with the least affection of a welcome
Give entertainment to the might of it,
Let God for ever keep it from my head
And make me as the poorest vassal is
That doth with awe and terror kneel to it !

There is a reconciliation, the Prince sits by his father's bed, and the King makes a speech of wise counsel and repentance. In such a solemn scene came the crown to Shakespeare's patriot King. Now follows one of the most dramatic crowning scenes in literature. The King is dead : long live the King ! Ancient Pistol hurries down to Gloucestershire. Falstaff sees himself the greatest man in England, the power behind the throne. Shakespeare sets him down, in one of his tensest scenes, at the gate of Westminster Abbey when the King comes by.

The crowd is waiting outside the Abbey for the King to pass, and near the door stand Falstaff, Shallow, and Pistol. Falstaff sets Master Shallow by him. He will make the King do him grace ; he will leer upon him as he comes by—and let them mark the look the King will give him! The King comes, and his old companions cannot restrain themselves from crying out:

God save thy grace, King Hal! my royal Hal!
The heavens thee guard and keep, most royal imp oj
*   fame!*
God, save thee, my sweet boy!
My King! my Jove! I speak to thee, my heart!

But Henry the Fifth is going to his crowning. He has done in a moment with his old days and his old ways. A few moments he pauses, long enough to break an old man's heart:

I know thee not, old man: fall to thy prayers;
How ill white hairs become a fool and jester . . .
Presume not that I am the thing I was,
For God doth know (so shall the world perceive)
That I have turned away my former self;
So will I those that kept me company.
When thou dost hear I am as I have been,
Approach me, and thou shalt be as thou wast,
The tutor and the feeder of my riots:
Till then I banish thee, on pain of death,
Not to come near our person by ten mile.

So our Master Englishman gives us the picture of the solemn hours of crowning; so King Henry the Fifth put away his wilder days and clothed himself with sanctity at the sight of the crown.

Crowned and throned, George the Sixth stands before his people, head of a long line of sixty kings reaching back to the Danes and Saxons. As his crown has changed, from dynasty to dynasty and from reign to reign, so his kingly powers have changed. He cannot do all that his ancestors could do, for it is the virtue of the British crown that while it gives its wearer supreme power it changes with the changing world, and fits into our modern times as it fitted into ancient time.

In any reign the crown is supreme, but its rights are never boundless. It has been the genius of our nation that it has preserved this ancient institution at its head, moulding it to its heart's desire yet strengthening it from age to age. When the crown has seemed too powerful its power has been curbed. It has not been the idea of our people that kings should rule over multitudes of men as if men were sheep and kings were gods. It is the proud distinction of our race that it has given the world the most astonishing example ever known of a monarchy flourishing like a tree with its roots in the hearts of its people. Beginning as masters of the people, our kings have become our servants, and it is because King George is the servant of his people that his crown is the safest on the earth. It is part of what we call the British Constitution, a thing not made with hands, unwritten and unread, yet still the very lifeblood of our people.

It is the invisible anchor of the British race. It enshrines the ideas of English-speaking people everywhere. It is what we believe and what we are, and it cannot be upset. When Mr Anthony Eden says at the League of Nations that we will not allow anyone to wrest our democracy from us, he means that we will not allow anyone to destroy the British Constitution, to rob us of our birthright, to interfere with our ways of life, our liberty, our right to say what we think. He means that we will not allow anyone to overthrow the institutions we have built up in this spirit of freedom and justice and equality for all. Although it does not exist in words, the British Constitution has five unshakable foundation stones. One is Magna Carta, which gave us parliaments and laws in the year 1215. One is the Habeas Corpus Act, which in 1679 gave us liberty of the person; Habeas Corpus means *have the body*, and by this act a body must be produced if it is alive. In 1701 the Act of Settlement made the crown the bulwark of Protestantism. In 1911 the Parliament Act established the supremacy of the House of Commons over the peers. In 1928 the Statute of Westminster made our great colonies into daughters no more, but sisters equal with the Motherland. So it is that the rock of British liberty has been built up from age to age, and it is in our blood and in our crown that none shall take these things away.

It is by curious ways at times that Crown and Parliament have been evenly balanced. The Houses of Parliament are still a royal palace, and Parliament is summoned and dissolved by Royal Proclamation. But the King may not enter while Parliament is sitting; never again can King George sit in his old place behind the clock. When the King sends his messenger to the House of Commons the House keeps Black Rod waiting until he has knocked three times, to show that Parliament can do as it pleases. When the King's speech is presented to the House the House turns to discuss some ordinary Bill, to show that it can keep the King waiting if it likes. In the Parliament of Jersey the bailiff's chair is six inches higher than the King's, to show the supremacy of the civil power. And yet Parliament cannot arrest the King. In the eyes of the law the

King can do no wrong. Parliament cannot even
arrest anyone in a royal palace or seize goods there.

The powers of the Crown and the Parliament have
been so delicately balanced through the centuries
that while neither is supreme neither can do without
the other. It is true that the King is answerable
to no power on earth for anything he does, but he
cannot make war as his ancestors could, he cannot forbid a law that Parliament has passed, he
cannot demand money except through Parliament,
he cannot dismiss a Government unless he is able
to replace it. It is not always written that he
cannot do these things ; sometimes it is the force
of custom only that restrains him.

And yet his power runs on where the power of
Parliament ends, for he rules over vast dominions in
which his ministers in Whitehall have no voice.
The Cabinet in London can no longer advise
the King on the affairs of the Dominions. It is
the Cabinet for the United Kingdom, for certain
colonies, and (for a little while) for India ; he is
king of all these and also of Australia, New Zealand,
Canada, South Africa.

That is the measure of the liberty that runs
through the British Empire. The people of its
dominions do as they will with no dictatorship.
The Empire has one king, but it no longer speaks
with one voice. Already Canada appoints her own
ambassador to Washington, Paris, and Tokyo.
South Africa has made it impossible for the Union
to be involved in war by the British Government
without its consent. Under the Locarno Treaty
for preserving peace in Europe the Dominions

secured the right to agree or to differ with the British Government.

So real is the change that has come about in the position of the Dominions that as King George the Fifth lay dying, and a Council of State was formed for an emergency, none of the Ministers present could be appointed to the Council, because it would have given the United Kingdom power and precedence over the Dominions. Before the Crown the Prime Minister of the United Kingdom is equal and no more with the Prime Minister of New Zealand. A solemn thing it is that the King should stand alone as ruler of those distant realms. The crown he wears has a significance for him that none of his ancestors (except for a few years his father) has known. He has a throne on every continent and for every continent he must be crowned.

More than a symbol is this glittering jewel with all its beauty and all its heritage : it is the anchor of the unity of the boundless spaces and the teeming millions of the British Empire.

THE THRONE

THIS royal throne of kings, this solemn grandeur that has grown about the Stone of Scone tucked away under the old chair in the Abbey, has been the seat of power of a thousand years of rulers. Dynasty after dynasty, Scottish kings and English, Plantagenet and Tudor, Stuart and Hanoverian, all have used the great stone enshrined in King Edward's Chair.

There are few things in the world more beautiful than our Crown, and few more simple than our Throne. Any one of us may see it almost any day ; we may leave a bus at Westminster and in a minute or two may be standing by the King's throne, his coronation chair.

It is more than six hundred years old and must have been a dazzling sight when Master Adams the goldsmith and Master Walter the painter delivered it up for the crowning of our first King Edward. It was made in the days when English craftsmanship was at its best, at the end of the 13th century. It was then that Salisbury Cathedral was set up with the loveliest spire in England crowning its magnificence. It was then that so many of the treasures of our churches were made, the glorious coloured windows that fill them with heavenly light, the illuminated manuscripts with the delicate beauty that thrills us still as we look at them, the carving in our cathedral choirs, with the marvellous canopies and pinnacles crowning the stalls. Then craftsmen were proud to be English, and they were artists to the finger tips. Master Adams and Master Walter made the King's Chair into a thing of beauty, adorning its surface with mosaic in coloured glass; painting its panels with a knight on horseback, a king with his feet on a lion, and a monster's head; working into it two small leopards carved and painted; and resting the whole chair on four carved lions.

Under the seat the old Stone of Scone is tucked away on a shelf, and we can see it, as we can see that other crowning stone at Kingston. Eight kings were crowned on the Kingston stone, yet it stands in the wind and the rain; the Stone of Scone is sheltered in the Abbey by the Confessor's tomb. Perhaps we may like the thought of these two stones that have seen so much of our nation's story, one still in the open street and one in our sacred place, but both the seat of kings, precious stones of the English people for a thousand years.

The Stone of Scone goes back in legend farther than we need follow it, for no man knows how old it is. But we know it was carried by a King of Scotland to the Abbey of Scone 1100 years ago, and that there it was used for 400 years for crowning kings. Our first King Edward overran Scotland in 1296, brought the stone away, and set it where it stands by the Confessor's shrine. It is said that the Scots were much annoyed, but we may believe that they were satisfied when a Scottish king followed the stone and was crowned King of England on it. For six hundred years and more the stone has rested in King Edward's chair, and only once has the chair been out of the Abbey in that time. Then it was taken across the road into Westminster Hall, where Cromwell sat in it to be installed as Lord Protector of the Commonwealth. It was the one break in our line of kings, but there was no break in the history of the chair.

It is not known that anyone has sat in it save Cromwell and our kings except one boy, Peter Abbott the chorister. His name is on the back ; he carved it there one summer's night when he slept in this chair. Shakespeare makes one of his characters say of a dream :

> Methought I sat in seat of majesty
> In the cathedral church of Westminster,
> And in that chair where kings and queens are crowned,

but Peter Abbott did sit in the chair, slept all night in it, and carved on the back with his penknife, *P. Abbott slept in this chair July 5, 1800.*

It is impressive to stand in the Abbey among our kings, with the Confessor and Henry the Fifth and Queen Elizabeth lying about us in their stately tombs, and to look on this chair in which so many kings have sat to be invested as sovereigns of this realm,

> This royal throne of kings, this sceptred isle,
> This earth of majesty, this seat of Mars,
> This other Eden, demi-paradise,
> This fortress built by Nature for herself
> Against infection and the hand of war,
> This happy breed of men, this little world,
> This precious stone set in the silver sea,
> This blessed plot, this earth, this realm, this England.

THE TWO GEORGES AND THE TWO ELIZABETHS

Perhaps there is nothing else we can look upon that has remained as we see it so near the very heart of England all this time. This old stone has been the seat of royal power at least since the year 850, and has been encased in this old oak as the seat of English kings since 1296. Half our kings have been crowned on it, half of that long line of sixty rulers belonging to ten dynasties—twenty Saxons and Danes, four Normans, eight Plantagenets, six Lancasters and Yorks, six Tudors, seven Stuarts, six Hanovers, and the three Kings of our own century, now the House of Windsor.

If we run down our line of kings to see what manner of men they were we may begin with one of the best of them all, Alfred the Great, whose blood runs in King George's veins. He is one of the heroic figures of all time, our national hero, who found England rent and torn and falling to pieces and welded its people into one nation, the freest in the world. He thought nothing of himself, but only of his people; he fought not for his own power, but for their glory.

Perhaps there has never been another man of whom it can be said that he was the bravest and wisest of all who were living in his day. He feared no man and no danger: if things went ill he never gave in; when things went well he strove to make them go better. He taught men to love peace and order and justice and mercy, and he taught them to fight that they might defend themselves against their foes. Learning he loved much more than arms. He founded schools and translated books and did his best to educate the priests so that they might educate the people. It was said that in his day a woman might walk across the land and no harm come to her.

Whatever may be said of other kings, no man has ever been known to speak a word of dispraise against King Alfred.

Wise and strong kings reigned after him, but in time came the evil days of Ethelred the Unready, when woe came upon England and King Sweyn of Denmark raided and ravaged the land. But the dying Sweyn gave England another great king, his son Canute. He was King of the Danes as well as of the English, a wise man and a valiant warrior, and he welded the Danes and the English into one people, though after him their kingdoms were severed again, for a descendant of Alfred, Edward the Confessor, came from Normandy to be King of England. A man of gentle spirit and great piety was this King Edward, without guile but without skill to govern, loving best of all the ways of monks and the foreign customs among which he had been brought up. When they laid him in the shrine he built at Westminster the English people chose Harold for their king, a shrewd and brave soldier ; but the nation was divided, and now came our first Conqueror, William of Normandy. Landing at Pevensey, where Julius Caesar had landed a thousand years before, he met Harold at the Battle of Hastings, conquered him, and laid his sword on an old stone altar that we may see and touch in the grounds of Battle Abbey.

If we think of Alfred as the founder of our nation, we must think of the Conqueror as the man who pulled it together and made it strong. Little enough did William care for right or justice in anything but his own will ; what he would have he would take at any cost, and woe to him who stood between the Duke and his desire. Yet his desires were not petty or

wanton ; for the most part they were the great
ambitions of a conqueror. He made all England
feel the stamp of his iron heel, and yet he loved
the wild deer as though he had been their father.
One of our great historians has said that the history
of England for eight centuries has been what it is
because this man was what he was. We owe to his
marvellous character and his masterly powers more
than we owe to Alfred, perhaps as much as we owe to
Cromwell. Strange kings we have had, and desperate men among them, but never one more desperate
than he.

When this grim man arrived at Pevensey he would
feel, no doubt, already like a conqueror as he landed
his hosts on the spot where Caesar's legions must have
stood. As the sun set on Hastings on that famous
night the king was slain, the English ranks were
broken, and the troops were scattered in the dark.
We are told that the Conqueror pitched his tent
on the spot where Harold fell, and sat down to
eat and drink among the dead. Saxon England was
over, Norman England was begun.

He knew that he was king at last. A little way off
in Rouen the gentle Matilda was pleading with the
powers of heaven that the day might be his ; but of
gentleness there was none in this tanner's daughter's
son. He was to sit on the throne of Alfred ; he was
to shape the destinies of the nation that was to lead
the world in freedom and humanity ; yet the first
thing he did as our conqueror was to refuse a grave to
our dead king. He cared nothing whether men loved
or hated him.

The fire of the old Vikings still burned in him. He
would rally his soldiers with a voice like a trumpet.

He would march strong and vigorous in front of fainting troops. He would work with his men as if he were one of them. Where he found no road he would make one, and would lay the stones with his own hands. Yet he was scornful and pitiless, and his cruelty knew no bounds. When the French king mocked at him he set the French border on fire and blazed its hamlets to the ground. When townsmen hung skins on their walls to mock at his lowly birth he cut off the hands and feet of his captives and flung them into the streets.

Such a man was he who marched from Hastings up to London, and his wonderful powers brought England to his feet. Kent, Winchester, and London bowed down to him ; in two months he was King. On Christmas Day they crowned him in the Abbey. There was some turmoil, for when the people acclaimed him King his men outside mistook the noise and, thinking it hostile, set fire to the houses, so that William left the Abbey to see his capital burning. But so tranquil was the city, so quiet was England, that in a few months the new King could return to Normandy.

For twenty-one years the Conqueror ruled in England, and they were years of impressive events. Ruthless and just, his hand was everywhere. He made the people prosperous. He gave them courts. He surveyed the country and prepared a Domesday Book of all who owned the land. He put an end to the slave trade that had been the shame of Bristol. He devastated two hundred thousand acres of Hampshire and planted the New Forest.

And yet, so strange are the facts of this world, this man of cruelty it was who abolished punishment by death. Only one execution stains his reign. Seven centuries before we gave up hanging children for breaking windows or stealing sixpences the Conqueror decreed that no man was to suffer death for any crime.

It was in these twenty-one years that there was sown the seed from which has sprung much of our national strength. It is one of our characteristics that we have our revolutions going on all the time ; instead of destroying our institutions we repair and strengthen their foundations. This source of our strength, says one of our great historians, is largely due to William. He saved our institutions by holding his despotic sway over them. He loved order so much that no price was too great to pay for it. He gave tranquillity to the land and set it on the way for a thousand years of history. He was largely what he was, no doubt, because he grew up at a time when murder and fire were the arguments most beloved at Court, but he stands out, for all his savagery, as a ruler who knew what he wanted and a statesman who knew how to rule.

Whatever there was of evil in the Conqueror was ten times over in William Rufus his son, who seized the throne and ruled so cruelly that men were glad when he fell dead in the New Forest, his heart pierced by a comrade's arrow. It was his younger brother who now became King Henry the First. Thinking mostly of himself, yet not a lover of war but loving the arts of peace (so that men called him Beauclerc the Scholar), he had wit to see that the king is strong who rules his people justly as well as firmly, and because he made this his great aim, because he shielded the common people from oppression, he was much beloved and called the Lion of Justice. He also pleased the English by taking a wife from the old royal house, so that in the veins of his children ran the blood of Alfred. When Henry died his daughter Matilda and his nephew Stephen fought for his kingdom, and, though Stephen won, the son of Matilda followed him on the throne and there was a mighty change. He was Henry the Second, our first Plantagenet, who was not only King of England but ruled half France.

He restored the foundations of good government which the evil days of Stephen had nearly destroyed. He was the very man to set right what had gone wrong. We can picture him with his sturdy figure, his red hair, his quick and fiery eyes, a man of furious energy, swift in judgment, swift in movement, never resting, never tiring, fearfully quick in wrath, and losing all control in moments of passion, yet not cruel or unforgiving to any foe who sought forgiveness.

In such a man the barons learned that they had met their master, and a master well worth serving. Henry dealt justice with an even and iron hand. He gave the people their first title to a national legislative assembly. With domains stretching from the Cheviots to the Pyrenees, he had England as his chief domain, but his travels brought him in touch with the greatest minds of his age and he proved a wise and learned king.

Perhaps most of us remember him because of Thomas Becket, first his Chancellor and then his Archbishop. The archbishop grew bold and quarrelled with the king, who in his bitterness cried out, " Is there none who will rid me of this pestilent priest ? " Misunderstanding him, four knights set out for Canterbury and slew Becket at the altar, a crime which filled the king with remorse and made him evermore a sorrowful man. Yet in his reign began the proud heritage of our common law, common to the whole kingdom, for Henry was first of all our kings to send out judges far and wide to hold assizes. His son was the boldest knight in Christendom, Richard Lionheart, who loved crusading more than ruling, yet gave England her first juries, whose duty was to fix the contributions men should make to pay for his crusading.

Of all the men who ever sat upon the throne the worst was Richard's brother John. He loved the quickest way of getting anything, however dark and foul it was. He surrendered the throne of England to the Pope and received it back as his vassal : but the very misdeeds of King John drove the people to unite, and at last the barons forced him at Runnymede to set his seal to Magna Carta, which laid it down for ever that no King of England has the right to override the law. " They have given me four and twenty over-kings " cried King John in his rage. It is said that he threw himself on the floor gnawing sticks and straws as he found himself helpless before the barons. But the Great Charter was established in one day, so low had King John fallen and so powerful were the barons with the people united behind them. The charter fixed places for trials and secured the even flow of justice. It insisted on the nation's right to refuse unjust taxation. It declared that no freeman should be seized or imprisoned or in any way brought to ruin save by legal judgment or by the law of the land. To no man should justice be sold or denied or delayed. In Salisbury Cathedral is the tomb of a man who was at Runnymede ; upstairs in the library is a copy of the charter that was made for him. In Tewkesbury Abbey is an ancient stone of one of the barons with a Latin inscription which means, *Magna Carta is the law and let the King look out !*

The evil John died in the midst of a civil war he made, and his little son of nine sat on the throne. He was in no wise fit to be a king, for though he was not evil like his father he managed always to do the wrong thing and suffered himself to be guided not by the wise men of England but by the Pope. And yet he had a long and troubled reign, the longest but two in our history. Some good came out of it, for England grew more united and the barons grew more English, and there arose the valiant spirit of Simon de Montfort, who compelled the king to call the first English Parliament, which sat in the chapter house at Westminster a few yards away from King Edward's chair.

It was King Edward the First who now came to the throne. He has been called the greatest of all the Plantagenets for the work he did in shaping the law and the Parliament. He codified our laws and united the nation at last. He curbed the power of the barons and called together the first Parliament in which all three states of the realm were represented. He conceded the right of the people to refuse taxation unless it came from Parliament ; it has remained ever since one of the first principles of the Constitution that there shall be no taxation without representation. He conquered the Welsh people and made his first son Prince of Wales. He conquered Scotland and brought the coronation stone from Scone to Westminster. He carried to the Abbey of Glastonbury

what he believed to be the bones of King Arthur
and Queen Guinevere. We can see the place where
he laid them in the green turf of the ruined abbey.

He died on his way to Scotland in the stormy days
of Robert Bruce and Bannockburn, but he had ruled
so well that the nation never far receded from the
heights to which he led it. His son Edward went on
his foolish way until he was dethroned and done to
death, and then came our third Edward who lived
for fifty years after his father's death, so that his
reign was the longest except three in all our history.
It is famous for the king's own prowess in battle,
for unhappily the greater part of his reign was
taken up in fighting for the crown of France. Though
Edward revived the glories of his grandfather's reign,
strengthened the law by creating magistrates in
every county, building up international trade and an
invincible fleet to maintain it, the war was his chief
concern.

War became a national industry, the only profes-
sion of the younger sons of nobles, the everyday
business of the yeoman. It was then that the
English bowmen sprang up and became for a century
the most redoubtable warriors in Europe. The men
who went from England to fight in France were for
the first time free men, on friendly terms with their
leaders, the kings and princes fighting with them.
The Black Prince, King Edward's son, the model
of the spirit of his age, was only sixteen when he
took a commanding part in the battle of Crécy, only
twenty-five when he won the vital victory of Poitiers
and brought home captive the King of France.

Yet it was not all a king's war. England was

proud of her victories, and Parliament voted
supplies. But the struggle was too much for the
nation's financial resources. The time of exhaustion
came, for England was plunged into the Hundred
Years' War. It was the time (the 14th century)
when our great cathedrals were rising in all their
stately glory, and the face of the land was being
crowned with churches and monuments of astonishing beauty. Chaucer was riding to Canterbury with
his pilgrims, befriended by John of Gaunt, the
Black Prince's brother. Suddenly the Black Death
swept through the land, the most appalling infliction
that had ever befallen our people, cutting the
population in two. Suddenly, too, came the revolt
of the peasants which marked the opening years of
the reign of Richard the Second, the Black Prince's
much-loved son, King of England in his teens.
Young Richard showed himself a lad of courage :
much better a man he was in the beginning of his
reign than in the ending of it. The peasants rose in
revolt against the idea that they should remain on
the estates where they were born and work all their
lives for low wages ; they claimed the right to serve
whom they would and to work their own land.
Richard rode into their midst as they clamoured
about him, so courageous was the spirit of this
youthful king. He grew up to love literature and
the arts, he was the generous patron of Chaucer, he
completed the great Westminster Hall which William
Rufus had begun. Yet it cannot be said that he was
every inch a king, for at the death of John of Gaunt
he seized his son's estates, so that their lawful
owner, Henry Bolingbroke, returned in anger from
his exile, gathered an army about him, and swept
the country with his followers.

> I weep for joy
> To stand upon my kingdom once again !
> Dear earth, I do salute thee with my hand,

said Richard coming back from his Irish war, but
soon he was weeping for anything but joy :

> Of comfort no man speak !
> Let's talk of graves, of worms and epitaphs ;
> Make dust our paper, and with rainy eyes
> Write sorrow on the bosom of the earth ;
> Our lands, our lives, and all are Bolingbroke's.

The king whose life began so proudly had brought
himself as low as any English king had ever stooped :

> What must the king do now ?   Must he submit ?
> The king shall do it.   Must he be deposed ?
> The king shall be contented.   Must he lose
> The name of king ?   O' God's name, let it go.
> I'll give my jewels for a set of beads,
> My gorgeous palace for a hermitage,
> My gay apparel for an almsman's gown,
> My figured goblets for a dish of wood,
> My sceptre for a palmer's walking-staff,
> My subjects for a pair of carvèd saints,
> And my large kingdom for a little grave,
> A little little grave, an obscure grave ;
> Or I'll be buried in the king's highway.

So, deposing Richard, came Bolingbroke, Henry
the Fourth, ending the Plantagenets and beginning
the House of Lancaster.   With no true right to the
throne, he sought the favour of the people, but his
reign was troubled, he was in the grip of disease,
and when he died in the Jerusalem chamber his
son reigned in his stead and became our famous

hero-king of Agincourt.   We know him best from
Shakespeare.   In Henry the Fourth Shakespeare
shows us Prince Henry sowing his wild oats, as we
say, mixing with bad companions and sharing the
life of low people, but in Henry the Fifth the poet
pays rich compensation for any injustice he may
have done the prince.   He holds him up to the
admiration of the world and makes him an heroic
figure, our patriot king.   Who can forget the scene
when Henry is walking about on the eve of Agincourt
when the English soldiers talk bluntly and plainly
to all who come, great and small ?   They grumble
and fight with equal zest ; they say what they think
without fear ; they will die for their country if they
must, but let the king beware on Judgment Day !
Then it is that the king, alone with the night, makes
that great speech, Upon the king.   He must bear
all, yet

> what have kings that privates have not too,
> Save ceremony, save general ceremony ?
> And what art thou, thou idol ceremony ? . . .
> Canst thou, when thou command'st the beggar's knee,
> Command the health of it ?   No, thou proud dream,
> That play'st so subtly with a king's repose,
> I am a king that find thee, and I know
> Tis not the balm, the sceptre, and the ball,
> The sword, the mace, the crown imperial,
> The intertissued robe of gold and pearl,
> The farcèd title running 'fore the king,
> The throne he sits on, nor the tide of pomp
> That beats upon the high shore of this world,
> No, not all these, thrice-gorgeous ceremony,
> Not all these, laid in bed majestical,
> Can sleep so soundly as the wretched slave,
> Who with a body filled and vacant mind . . .
> Sleeps in Elysium. . . .

Who does not thrill as he reads St Crispin's day, which goes on resounding through the ages as one of the noblest speeches ever spoken by a king ? We feel that Henry really felt he was a brother with his soldiers. He raised himself to a great height of power from which he has never since fallen in the hearts of the people. Yet if we forget Shakespeare and judge him by the verdict of history we must remember that Henry should not have gone to France in search of a crown, and that the effects of the war were bad for France and England too. He won immortal fame at Agincourt and conquered half the realm of France, but in the end his people called him home, fearing to become a colony of France, and all that he had won was lost in the days of the son who followed him, Henry the Sixth, who grew up to be like a harmless well-meaning shadow, a ruler who spent his life in doing little more than building colleges while the warring families fought for the controlling government.

In his reign began the Wars of the Roses, beginning with the plucking of roses as badges in Temple Gardens, for Prince Edward the Fourth of the House of York won a great victory and proclaimed himself king as Edward the Fourth. He sat insecurely on the throne, though he was a wonderfully brilliant soldier and never lost a battle. He was indolent and reckless, gifted but selfish, caring little for anything now that he had won the crown. He left his throne to his young son, but the poor prince was never to reign, for he was one of the two little brothers who were suffocated in the Tower to make way for their uncle as Richard the Third. Little time need we waste on him, wading through blood to the throne, keeping it by terror, trusting no man and trusted by none, friend today and foe tomorrow. In the end young Henry Richmond of the House of Lancaster came from exile to rid the country of this usurper, and they met at Bosworth Field. The day was done, the dog was dead, says Shakespeare in his brief report of the battle which brought into England the famous Tudor dynasty with Henry the Seventh, grandson of a Welsh squire who had married the widow of Henry the Fifth.

It was the end of the Wars of the Roses and the beginning of the most famous dynasty in our long line of kings. Henry climbed to the throne by the sheer force of his victory, for he was crafty and could get what he wanted, an unpleasant king in many ways but mostly with the welfare of the country at heart, and he gave it back the peace and order which had been so terribly disturbed. By marrying a princess of the House of York he united the warring factions. He promoted trade and manufactures. He gave us a good merchant navy. He satisfied the Scots by giving his daughter in marriage to the Scottish king. He gave Henry Cabot ten pounds for finding a continent which proved to be North America.

Now it is that there comes into our English scene that marvellous king of the House of Tudor, Henry the Eighth.

He was one of the most astonishing men who have appeared in history, a man of the stamp of the Conqueror though four centuries stood between them. It has been said that he approached as near the ideal standard of perfect wickedness as human frailty will allow, and yet he was a great king if we measure him by the events of his reign. He found himself firm on his throne with plenty of money in his treasury. He was an accomplished prince, well read, skilled in music, and a great athlete. He was generous in his ways. Yet behind all this show he was detestably selfish, though part of his selfishness was really ambition, the desire to have the reputation of a great king and to be ruling over a great people. He was a shrewd judge of men and gathered about him the most remarkable court an English monarch had ever known. We know him from Holbein's pictures, from Sir Thomas More's letters, and from Erasmus (the wisest man in Europe in his day), and we know him well from Shakespeare. He had two great ministers in his reign, Thomas Wolsey and Thomas Cromwell, each of whom served him with unsparing zeal, taking upon themselves the blame for whatever he did that was unpopular, only to be flung on one side when they had served his turn. It was the same with his wives; he had six, most of whom he beheaded or put away when he was tired of them. There is much that is true in the spirit of Shakespeare's play of this astounding man.

The great business of his reign was the quarrel with the Pope, who at first refused to help him to put away Catherine of Aragon, his faithful wife; for this King Henry decided that the Pope's authority should be recognised no more in England, but that the king should be ruler of the Church. He destroyed the monasteries; his creature Thomas Cromwell shattered great churches and abbeys into ruin, and Henry seized the rich estates the Church had built up for centuries. Out of all this came the great Reformation and the establishment of Protestantism in England. It may be true, as Henry said, that monks were living evil lives, but so was he, and it was not for the Reformation or for Protestantism that Henry and his servant Cromwell destroyed the monasteries ; it was to enrich the king and give him great estates to distribute to his friends.

This remarkable man left three remarkable children, all of whom came to the throne. They were Mary Tudor, Edward the Sixth, and our famous Queen Elizabeth. They ruled for more than half a century, the tragic fourteen days of Lady Jane Grey coming between them. First came Edward the Sixth, a delicate little fellow extraordinarily clever ; he reigned for six years and was succeeded by his sister Mary. Hers was the bitterest short reign in all our history. She was the daughter of Henry the Eighth's faithful Catherine, and, though her reign of terror makes us shudder as we read, it was not cruelty but a misguided devotion that led her to send 300 innocent people to the stake. She was not cruel in herself ; she was merciful to her personal enemies, but she felt it wrong to be merciful to the enemies of her faith. She was a loyal Roman Catholic, and believed that in burning the bodies of Protestants she was saving their souls and sending them to heaven.

There have been few more pitiful figures in the history of England than Catherine of Aragon's daughter, who felt that she was serving her faith by burning those who did not follow it. She it was who burned Latimer and Ridley, so that from her five years of terror come those immortal words which will never pass away :

Be of good cheer, Master Ridley, we shall this day light such a candle in England as I trust by God's grace shall never be put out.

Now came to the throne of England perhaps the cleverest woman who ever sat on a throne in the world, Elizabeth. Our Golden Age had come. It was still a cruel world, with the effects of generations of war still working in men's minds, with the memory of generations in which kings had beheaded their enemies (or their friends) as a matter of course, with the throne rarely free from conspiracies and plots ; and it was a world so strange that Mary Tudor, Queen of England, married England's greatest enemy, King Philip of Spain.

Happily it did not happen that England became a colony of Spain under Mary ; it did happen, instead, that under Elizabeth Philip's great Armada, sent to destroy us, was sent itself to destruction, and England took the place of Spain as mistress of the seas. Our explorers opened the gates of the world ; our seamen made the sea safe for our ships. They were the days of Francis Drake and Walter Raleigh, the days of all those famous Devon men who sailed the seas and found new lands and established our world trade. They were the days of Edmund Spenser and Philip Sidney and Shakespeare. There has never been a generation like it, and it must seem to us as something more than a coincidence that there should have been on the throne a woman like Elizabeth at the time when England was at its height of fame and intellectual power. On the throne sat one of the most brilliant women the world has ever known, and in her capital and in her court was the most brilliant company of spirits that ever came together in our land.

Elizabeth was clever enough to know that Philip meant to crush the Reformation and to strike down Protestantism ; she knew that he intended to turn against England when he had disposed of his

5

Protestant subjects in Holland.   One of the loveliest
bronze monuments in England is in the Tate Gallery,
showing Elizabeth and Philip sitting at a game of
chess with the world their chessboard.   It was like
that, but Elizabeth did not mean to lose the game.
She did not mean England to fight Spain till England
was strong enough to be sure of winning, and she
spent half her reign in secretly helping Holland and
quietly doing all the damage she could to Spain.

All that time she was ruling England firmly, seeing
that the men through whom she ruled were honest
above all.   She stood by her servants and they stood
by her, though she gave her ministers a hard time,
scolding them like a fishwife and boxing their ears if
they did not do as she chose.   After all her waiting
the time came for her final move in the game of chess,
and her victory resounded through the world.   She
was vain ; she would forget that she was growing old.
She refused to go to bed to die until the very end.
But all her energies and all her plottings and all her
dreams were for her country, and when she died,
angry that her time had come, England was the
greatest nation in the world.

It was now that a king came down from Scotland
to sit on the Stone of Scone.   He was James Stuart,
grandson of the grandson of Henry the Seventh.   It
was a king of France who called him the wisest fool
in Christendom, by which he meant that James the
First had much learning and could argue with keen
wit, but through his cunning he always overreached
himself.   It is the bitterest memory of his reign that
he betrayed Sir Walter Raleigh to the King of Spain,
so that the head of the founder of the British Empire
fell outside the Abbey walls.   James was very much

a coward, allowing himself to be controlled by favourites who took his fancy but were not to be trusted. Perhaps there never was a king who thought so much as he of his kingly office, which he believed to have been given him by God ; certainly there never was an English king on whom the kingly office sat so absurdly, who was so hopelessly un-majestical, and whose kingcraft did worse service to the crown. Not that it brought disaster upon him, but that it sowed the seed of the harvest whose bitterness his son Charles Stuart was to reap.

It is pathetic to see King Charles looking from the canvas of Van Dyck and to remember his tragic figure in the history book. He was as blameless as the strictest Puritan in his private life. He must have been a delightful companion for his friends. At home he was affectionate and religious. Those who knew most of him felt most sorrowful about him, for he was a man of great piety and deep faith. But with all these noble qualities Charles was a bad king. His mournful and dignified figure was utterly unlike the grotesque figure of his father, but some of his father's qualities he had, and many of his beliefs. He was obstinate, confident in his own cunning, unable to choose wise counsellors, and his father had stamped indelibly on his mind the belief in the divine right of a king to do as he pleased.

It was this that brought disaster on King Charles. He thought kings were not bound to keep their word, that they could make a pledge and break it, that they could do as they liked with their people. He believed that because he was king by the will of God he must be right in everything he did, and that if he could not get his way honestly it was right for him to get it dishonestly. What he wanted was usually what most of his subjects did not want, so that the people were forced into rebellion, and when they were victorious Charles would try to win over one group or another by making promises he never meant to keep. His word could not be trusted. Blameless as a man, he was without honour as a king, and he drove the nation to despair.

The rise of Oliver Cromwell, the strongest man of his age, the greatest military genius England has ever known, divided the nation into two camps, and Charles was faced with a man who was more than his master, who believed in God as much as he, whose word was his bond, and whose faith was his secret strength. When it was clear that the king could not be trusted there was no way but his death, and one winter's morning when the snow was falling the king walked through St James's Park to Whitehall Palace and died with the word *Remember* on his lips.

Oliver Cromwell ruled the Commonwealth for ten years. Installed as Protector while sitting in King Edward's Chair in Westminster Hall, he raised England to a dignity she had never known before. He maintained law and justice and made the nation peaceful at home and feared abroad. He was a Dictator, but he ruled the country in the sight of God, in whom he believed above all, and it was by his character and his honesty that he ruled the land until he died. Then there being none to follow him, no man strong enough to be Dictator, Charles Stuart's son reigned as Charles the Second. He cared much for himself and little for his country. He tried to work out plans to make the throne independent of Parliament without running any risk. For his own purposes he sold his country to the King of France, pledging himself to rule England, as far as he could without being found out, in accordance with the French king's wishes. He had none of the finer qualities of his father, and his court was as dissolute as himself. He dug up Cromwell's bones in the Abbey and hung his body on Tyburn and set his head on a pike outside Westminster Hall, where it remained for over twenty years ; there it was seen by Pepys, who went home and wrote in his diary that he did see this thing and felt it an indignity for so great a man.

Charles the Second's place was taken by his brother James, who was not clever enough to conceal his plans for making himself an absolute king, for setting the laws at naught and for forcing the Roman Catholic faith on the country at the risk of his crown. He not only risked his crown but lost it, and with the country on the verge of civil war James fled to the Continent, and the crown was offered to the head of the Dutch Republic, whose mother was a Stuart and whose wife was King James's eldest child. William and Mary ruled for thirteen years, he proving an excellent king and making the good of the State his aim, and they were followed by Queen Anne, whose reign is remembered for the astonishing victories of the Duke of Marlborough against the French. When she died the nation was tired of Stuarts and turned to the German House of Hanover for another line of kings.

So it was that the great-grandson of James the First became our George the First, though he could not speak the language of our people and cared little about England, but left the country to govern itself through Parliament. Three Georges followed, the second counting little, the third counting much, losing America by his obstinacy and breaking down in body and mind towards the close of his long reign of sixty years. George the Fourth was called the First Gentleman in Europe without the slightest reason, for no man honoured him and the country was glad to have his brother, the bluff and honest sailor, as William the Fourth. He reigned a little while and was followed by Queen Victoria, who lived into our century, reigning for 63 years and more. It was the longest reign in England's history, the greatest period of invention and discovery and learning ever known in the world. It saw the beginning of the great transformation of the life of mankind—the quickening of transport, the coming of industrial power, the age of steam and electricity. In literature and art the Victorian Era was unmatched since the days of Elizabeth. In science it was the beginning of the great wonders of our time. It saw the dawn of travel on a scale that had never been dreamed of. It taught the world the laws of health and set men on the way to the conquest of disease. It added millions of square miles to the British Empire and gave the Empire freedom. It established free education and made this country the land of matchless opportunity and incalculable wealth.

The twentieth century was only about twenty days old when Edward the Seventh came to the throne, and he reigned for ten eventful years. He sought to build up friendship between the European nations, especially between the British and the German peoples, and he is remembered as Edward the Peacemaker.

Now into the history of our throne comes the most beloved king this generation of the world has seen. He was known to all who read this book, and at his Silver Jubilee was the central figure of the most remarkable outpouring of affection that any land has known. Night after night a great multitude no man could number would gather outside his palace and call him to the balcony; and the King would come. The twenty-five years of King George's reign were crowded with momentous events at home and abroad, and through them all he moved as a man whose one desire was to be of service to his people and a friend to all mankind. It was his genius that he made anyone at home with him, whether proud Indian princes, dusky potentates from the half-civilised parts of the Empire, visitors from other lands, or the homeliest citizen who found himself in the king's company. One of the last subjects he spoke to was the butcher's boy.

He never lost touch with his people, and through the war he shared alike with them in danger and privation. He gave up all luxuries and lived the simple life; he lived as in the ranks with all of us. He became a total abstainer for the duration of the war, being in this greater and more self-sacrificing than his Parliament. He became a kind of chief citizen rather than a king in the mind of the foreign peoples passing through London in those days. They wandered by Buckingham Palace in admiration for the king who was on rations.

He had travelled more than any other king, and knew so well the wisdom of a knowledge of the world that he sent his son to follow in his steps. He was the first king to know the British Empire. He had opened the first Parliament in the world with a whole continent for its constituency. He did his utmost to strengthen the weakening loyalty of Ireland, and summoned the political parties to Buckingham Palace for this purpose at the beginning of his reign. No reign had ever begun amid so great political turmoil, but King George, faced with the necessity for making stern and often painful decisions, made them so that no ill-feeling could exist among the bitterest partisans.

He was the first king to broadcast, and every Christmas he spoke to his people throughout the world. No king's voice had ever been so well known as his ; none till his had been heard throughout the world. It was by the mysterious voice that runs through space that the news came to his people that the reign of King George was over. Never before had the BBC sent out such a sorrowful piece of news to the British people as that now famous bulletin :

The King's life is moving
peacefully towards its close.

It came about half-past nine at night, and from then till midnight there were tears in every home as the people waited. The world was greatly moved. There was a minute of silence in Westminster Abbey, prayer at Canterbury Cathedral and at the Wall of Wailing in Jerusalem, and far away in Virginia the Speaker of the Parliament sent a message that the daughter had not wandered so far from the mother that they could not join their prayers with those of the English people. At that solemn midnight, with the memory of the unparalleled scenes of the Silver Jubilee fresh in the public mind, the best king who

ever ruled the British people passed away in his
country home at Sandringham. If we would write
his epitaph it would be hard to find a better one than
these few moving sentences in his first broadcast
speech to the Empire :

*To arrive at a reasoned tranquillity within our
borders ; to regain prosperity without self-seeking ;
and to carry with us those whom the burden of past
years has disheartened or overborne—my life's aim
has been to serve as I might towards those ends.*

In the last broadcast of all, only a week or two
before the end, came those words which still seemed
to be ringing in our ears in that midnight hour—
that he could never forget the great offering of love
for himself and his Queen at the Jubilee, and that
it was good to think that our family of peoples
was at peace with all nations, friend of all and
enemy of none.

King Edward for a few months followed his father,
and of his reign it is for Time to tell. Of his brother
George the Sixth, who followed him (three kings in
the year 1936), all the world knows that his promise
is as bright as a summer's day and all his people
greet him with affection and wish him well.

THE LAND

WHETHER we think of its beauty, or its history, or the character of its people or of their achievements, our Island has no match beneath the sun.

It is a comfortable little land as we walk about it, yet what a tale it tells! If we go back a hundred years it is like a miracle, for it has been at the head of mankind in that march to knowledge and power which has made the Twentieth Century the most remarkable since the beginning of the world. If we go back a thousand years we can hardly believe the story of what has happened in these islands. If we go back a million years the tale is something that staggers the wisest man alive. For all our mists and rains, our placid rivers and our gleaming lakes, our mountains smiling in their modest majesty, our little hills clapping their hands, our valleys with their ever green carpets, these islands were moulded and shaped by Nature in her angriest moods.

Time, and the ocean, and some fostering star
In high cabal have made us what we are,

says William Watson. It is true. We have been under the sea. We have been covered with ice. We have been strewn with the fire of volcanoes. We have been a land of great forests. We have been a jungle of wild beasts. We have been thrust up and thrust down. We have been linked by a land

bridge to Europe.   If we are Freedom's Own Island,
as Emerson says, we certainly were first of all
Nature's Own Island.

We were a land of fiery volcanoes, of earthquakes
that split the earth for hundreds of miles.   We have
our scars to show, and the cones of our dead
volcanoes.   Edinburgh Castle, sitting on its rock
and looking down on Princes Street, is resting on a
dead volcano.   Snowdon was in flame for ages.
Cader Idris, Scafell, Helvellyn, Dartmoor, and the
Cornish hills were all on fire, centres of volcanic
energy, in the long ages when these islands were
settling down and waiting for their age of peace.
Snowdon, rising in stately splendour 3570 feet above
the sea, once lay at the bottom of a valley.   Truly
the valleys have been exalted and the heights
made low.

If we would take a walk down the steps of Time
with our feet on the rocks in the order in which they
were laid down, we need not leave these islands, for
here is possible an experience which comes to no
traveller anywhere else in the world.   Here and
there in the world the first rocks laid down have come
to the surface, brought up by the terrific twistings
and pressures of the earth in the days when our
planet was shaping ; and it seems like a miracle
that we may start from London and cross the
country so that we walk on the rocks in the order
in which they were made, from the newest to the
oldest, each step millions of years older than the one
before.   We cross London's bed of clay, over the
Chilterns with their chalk, to Edgehill with its
oolites and its fossil lizards, through the Midland
coalfields to Shropshire with its Silurian rocks at

Wenlock Edge, past Shrewsbury to the rocks with not one sign of life, and on to Snowdon formed by fire. When at last our world had settled, a curious thing had happened that should thrill the imagination of the English-speaking race. If we take a globe of the world and arrange it so that we see the greatest land-mass we can look upon, *our Island is set in the very midst of it.*

But all that is very long ago, before men and kings were thought of. Let us look round our little land as a few centuries have made it, with its famous towns and its lovely villages, and all its wonder packed in so little space. She is, as Shakespeare said, like a little body with a mighty heart. Ages have made our valleys, and they are like so many secret places with their hidden treasure, murmuring streams, old mills, sleepy hollows, green meadows, deep gorges, mysterious caverns, footpaths trodden for a thousand years. Our green carpet is the loveliest in the world ; never does the traveller forget the green fields of England. Our rivers flow through the fairest landscapes. Our little lanes bring us to scenes unmatched in any country in the world. Our wondrous coast, set in a silver sea, has white cliffs, granite walls, and golden sands. Our hills bring us to great solitudes with not an echo of the noisy world. Our moors and wolds give us thrilling suggestions of the spacious loneliness of greater lands. Our woods and forests with their majestic avenues are like ancient shrines of silence.

How many little worlds we can count in this land we may work out for ourselves, but certainly we have half a dozen Englands, and perhaps as many Scotlands, and perhaps as many types in Wales.

We have Industrial England, teeming with mines and mills and factories and sending their products to the ends of the world. We have Historic England, with its scenes of the great events that have shaped our destiny. We have Cathedral England, with ancient splendour that holds us spellbound. We have the Poet's England, for ever immortal. We have the Artist's England, known in pictures everywhere. We have Rural England, with Nature's lovely little nooks that not all the spoilers of the country have been able to destroy. If we bring them all together we have the Traveller's England, drawing pilgrims from every land in search of all these things. Again and again the traveller returns. The wonders of America do not keep him away. The distance from Australia is no barrier. The marvels of India cannot quench the desire to see our English villages. When East comes West it is England the pilgrim will not miss. It stirs in the page of history and it thrills in the heart of man.

To those who go about our land with understanding it is like a living book. Here are still the ancient trackways older than the empires of the world. Here are still the ancient temples, the Westminster Abbeys of a forgotten race. Here are the citadels of men in the days when they fought the lion and the bear with sticks and stones. Here are their workshops, their settlements, the little things they left about. We may pick up chippings from their flints, the bones from their meals, the tools with which they worked, charcoal from the fires they made. We find the first pictures they drew, the first tools they shaped, the first simple shrines they set up to worship some mysterious power they could not understand. We find ivory engraved with fine tools, a pendant made from a mammoth's tusk as thin as a postcard with a hole suggesting that a lady of the caves had worn it. Here twenty thousand years ago there were artists in the land, in the days when men could walk from the banks of the Thames to the banks of the Seine.

If we walk about the Wiltshire Downs we find them strewn with the graves of unknown warriors, buried before our history began. There is no more pathetic scene in England than that long stretch of green from Avebury down to Stonehenge, with thousands of graves bearing poignant witness to the desire of these primitive people to lay their warriors as near to Stonehenge as they could, for it was their famous shrine. We find in Wiltshire also not only their graves but their temples, temples of wood and stone, for in the last years of the reign of George the Fifth a flying man, looking down from the sky over Wiltshire, found the signs of a timbered temple older than the stones of Stonehenge. He found a ring of wheat that was higher than the rest, and on the reason being looked for men found 160 holes cut in the chalk with piles of wood in them. They were the foundations of a temple forty centuries ago. Another has been found at Bleasdale in Lancashire, and the timbers have been preserved in the great museum at Preston, the oldest known timbers in the world.

So we find everywhere about us some witness of the past. If we come to our historic days, with Caesar at the gate, we find his Roman walls still standing impressively at Pevensey, the cobbles of his Watling Street at Richborough, and everywhere throughout the land we find the work of his builders and the mark of his legions. In York we may see a Roman lady's hair as it lay in her coffin on the day they laid her in her grave. At Rochester we may see the mark of Roman chariot wheels, and the timbers of a Roman bridge. On the hilltop where this book is written is the mark of a little dog's paw as it ran across a Roman tile which was hardening in the sun. At Colchester is a Roman temple built to a god of the sun before there was a Christian church in England. We have miles of Roman walls, a Roman city covered by a wheatfield, and thousands of lovely things the Romans left behind when they hurried from their British colony.

After the Romans the Saxons, and their monuments are everywhere. We have a church they built across a Roman fort looking out to the North Sea. We have a church still standing with the timbered walls they built. Very fascinating are their quaint little doorways and windows, and the queer carvings of their craftsmen. We have some of the sundials with which they told the time, the fonts at which they christened their little ones, the jewels they gave their women, the pictures they painted, and the manuscripts they wrote. It would be possible to bring together a thousand wonderful things that have come down to us from Saxon England.

And then there came a wondrous change, for William the Conqueror sailed from Normandy and stood where Caesar stood, at Pevensey. It was the end of Saxon England, and a mighty transformation came over the land. The Normans built their forts and castles and churches, and we wonder still at these stupendous places—their great cathedral arches, their castle gateways, their majestic keeps, their wonderful towers. They are gigantic and impressive, the first magnificent monuments that have survived in their full glory. But more than all perhaps we are astonished by the beautiful work of the Norman craftsmen; not only strength but beauty they put into all they did. Their work has lasted 800 years and it will stand for thousands more.

But who shall describe the loveliness of the work of the English builders who followed on ? We see it beginning as the Norman influence passed away. We see the great round arches becoming pointed. In doorways and windows and cathedral aisles the pointed Gothic stones appear. The Englishman is at work ; he has learned his lesson and has improved on his masters. He could build higher and better and with a beauty the Norman could not dream of, sending his spires up high, carving his stones with the delicacy of a jewel, covering the land with his enchanting spectacles.

In the 13th century he was feeling his way ; in the next he was boldly decorating his columns and doorways ; in the 15th century he rose triumphant to the skies. When we see a great 15th-century church we see the best thing that our builders have set up on the earth. If we would see one of the 13th century we go to Salisbury ; for the 14th we go to Exeter ; for the 15th to Gloucester ; but we may see all these at the end of our little lanes, in one of those villages of which we have ten thousand with something old, or beautiful, or historic, or quaint, or with some interesting link with the past. We have thousands of villages older than the United States, and all about our countryside are monuments

of the days before America was heard of. On the wall of a church is often found a dial scratched in stone with the rays that radiate from a central hole ; ages ago they were the people's clocks. Often at a manor house we may see a dovecot centuries old with resting-places for hundreds of thousands of doves ; they come from the days when there was no food to keep our cattle alive in winter, so that they were slaughtered, and the lord of the manor or the priest kept doves for food. Sometimes we see a curious door high up in a tower ; it comes from the days when the tower was a place of refuge from enemies and the people would run up with a ladder. Often we see the old tithe barn, perhaps in the form of a cross and inside with a kind of nave and transept; it is the place where the faithful took their tithe, their tenth, to the church, the farmer paying in wheat. More thrilling than all, perhaps, is a little thing that looks so dull, the iron staple still found in hundreds of our fonts. It tells of the days when men still believed in witches and the font was locked against them lest they should steal the holy water.

What do we not find in this ancient land ? We have all seen the stocks for the village ne'er-do-well, and the mounting-stones for lords and ladies riding to church on Sunday, but perhaps not all of us have seen the niches for beehives in old cottages ; the ice-houses underground in which the rich kept ice all through the summer ; the odd little marks the mason carved on the stone when he finished his work ; the consecration cross where the bishop put his hand on consecration day ; the candleholders in the pews of churches and the hourglass in the pulpit ; the long hook for drawing burning thatch from roofs ; the little cell of the anchorite, who would shut himself into it and live walled up for the rest of his life gazing on the altar of the church. All these we may see, curious witnesses of the strange story of the past.

It has happened in our time that an Englishman has flown fifty thousand feet high above our country, and seen in a glance all England below London, from the landing-place of our ancestors on the Kent coast to King Arthur's Castle at Tintagel and the sharp granite crags of Land's End. It is not a wild dream to think that the day will come when a man will fly beyond this dazzling height and see at one glance all our island—or all our islands. Some of them will be too small for him to see from his throne in the heavens, for we have more islands than any traveller has ever visited, five thousand of them. There are a hundred Shetland Islands and nearly a hundred Orkneys, though only a quarter of them have living people on them. There are five hundred islands in the Hebrides with one in five inhabited. There are dozens of Channel Islands and a hundred and forty Scillies. The farthest island north of Scotland is farther from Edinburgh than Edinburgh is from London. Some of our islands are as near to Norway as to Scotland ; even Shetland is farther from London than London is from Switzerland.

But the island our flying man would look on is the great island a thousand miles round in which lie England and Wales and Scotland. Let us imagine what he would see if his eye could run quickly round.

He would see the great gateway of England at Dover, with the mysterious heights of the castle and the Roman lighthouse, and his eye would run up that historic coast, past the Roman walls of Richborough, on to Ebbsfleet, where the first Englishman landed, and then to Canterbury with its medieval walls and the mother cathedral of English-speaking Christendom. Up Kent his eye would run, between the North Downs and the marshes of the Thames, to Chatham with the Medway home of the British fleet, to Rochester with its wonderful Norman spectacle indoors and out, on to Gravesend and across to Tilbury, on into East Anglia through Colchester, the town of Shakespeare's Cymbeline, of proud Boadicea and brave Caractacus, the town with the Roman walls and the Norman castle and the Saxon church.

He would see Bury St Edmunds with the massive gateway leading into the garden where the barons swore on the altar that King John should do their will, and then would come Norwich, with Sir Thomas Erpingham in the cathedral, and the Norman castle on the hill, and the Norfolk Broads not far away. Then on to Boston, with the proudest church tower in England on the banks of the Witham, across the Lincolnshire fens, past Lincoln Cathedral which John Ruskin thought the greatest piece of architecture in the land, up into Yorkshire, with millions of people, and more acres than there are letters in the Bible, and room to put all London and nine other counties in. Its moors rise 1700 feet above the sea. It is the cradle of our English poetry. It has hundreds of churches in which twenty-five generations of people have been christened or married or laid to rest. It was the home of Captain Cook, who made our Empire possible by making life safe at sea. It has the oldest town in England and a minster that holds us spellbound with half an acre of old glass in its windows, more than all the rest

of England put together. Northward our flying
man's eye would fall on Durham, and would see, rising
on a rock from the river, one of the noblest things
the hands of man have made upon the earth,
Durham Cathedral. At one end lies Cuthbert, who
was buried with a little red book we may see at
Stonyhurst, and at the other end lies Bede, who
wrote the life of Cuthbert, and was buried with a
ring which we may see in this cathedral.

Now the airman's glance would run to Newcastle,
with all the shipping on the Tyne ; he would look
down on the seventy-mile wall the Romans built to
keep back the Scots ; and then, with a wondrous
sweep, all Scotland would be stretched before him—
Edinburgh and Glasgow, Stirling with the Wallace
Tower and Dunfermline with the grave of Bruce,
Perth and Aberdeen, the lovely country round
Balmoral, the mountains and the moors, the lochs
and bens, the home of Livingstone at Blantyre, the
home and grave of Scott, Rosslyn Chapel like
nothing else in our island, the great Forth Bridge, the
Clyde, and the ruined walls of Melrose whose shadows
fall over the heart of Robert Bruce. Coming down
on the west, his quick glance would take in Carlisle,
and the lovely English lakes where Wordsworth lived
and Ruskin died, and then in a moment his eye would
fall on Liverpool, city of dreams and splendour, with
its wonderful spectacle by the Mersey and the
wonderful highway under it, with the great plateau
of St George's Hall crowning the city, and two
cathedrals rising, one to be the biggest in the world
and one with an east window its great lady chapel
could pass through. Now comes Chester, the most
complete walled town in England, and then the
mountains of Wales and Carnarvon Castle, and soon

we are at Shrewsbury and on our way to captivating
Ludlow, beautiful with its black and white fronts,
and the great castle where Philip Sidney played as a
boy and John Milton came as a man to see his Comus
first produced.

The view now comes to Monmouth, where Henry
of Agincourt was born, and the matchless valley of
the Wye, with Tintern Abbey like a sentinel on the
road to heaven. Here is Worcester and here is
Cheltenham, and here is the lovely street of Cirencester
with a church magnificent at the top and precious
Roman monuments not far away. Then this eye in
the sky would fall on Gloucester, with the cathedral
in which two great ideas of English building were
born, and forty miles of natural splendour lower
down stands Bristol, the city set on a hill that can
never be hid in the world. It is part of English
history. Another glance and the flying man is
looking down on Bath, built about the ruins of a
Roman city, with possessions unequalled and history
almost past belief. Now comes the lovely town of
Wells, with the moated palace of the bishop, a
cathedral like no other, a thousand feet of columns
in its chapter house, and a mile of exquisite carving
in its naves and aisles. Here is Somerset with its
towers of splendour, with the glory of Exmoor and
the Mendips, and Devon with its comfortable
villages, its incomparable Clovelly, its famous
Bideford, and the homes of our great seamen.

This eye that is seeing all England has come to our
Atlantic coast with the sea beating in vain against
the granite walls of Cornwall, and soon comes Exeter
within its gaze, with a cathedral in which the
clustered piers rise like trees in a forest, into which

its builders seem to have put all the beauty of Devon, its little gems of loveliness, its sweeping majesty. Looking down on Exeter the flying man would see Dartmoor on one side and Exmoor on the other, and a little way off the farmhouse Sir Walter Raleigh was born in, and Plymouth Hoe where Drake played bowls, from where the Mayflower sailed.   A little way east would be Dorset, with the old town of Dorchester and Maiden Castle older than history, and soon his eye would fall on Salisbury and Winchester, the one with the loveliest spire in England, the other with the dust of Alfred and Canute, the stupendous Norman transepts and the lovely little chantries, and the famous cloisters of great beauty in memory of 500 Winchester boys who went to the war and never came back.   Then Southampton with the old walls and the marvellous docks, and Portchester Castle at Portsmouth with a Roman wall half-a-mile round.

Looking from Hampshire into Sussex, one of the specks he would see would be Chichester Cathedral, elegant and beautiful, the only ancient cathedral visible from the sea. Along the coast lie Brighton and Lewes, Eastbourne with its magnificent sea front, Hastings with its famous memory and its ruined castle, Battle Abbey where Saxon England ended and Norman England began ;   and the spectator in the clouds would see the way to London through Surrey, up Guildford's famous street and through Croydon, the flying man's Charing Cross.

But in the heart of this great ring round England lies that middle England we have missed : Hertfordshire with St Albans, city of the Romans and the Normans and our first martyr ; Bunyan's Bedfordshire and Cromwell's Huntingdon, Cambridge in all its glory, Ely with its famous tower and Peterborough with its wonderful nave ; Leicester with the ruins of the abbey where Wolsey came to die ; Nottingham with its castle on the hill, the domed town hall, and the university with its lily tower ; Derbyshire with Dovedale, the most exquisite little valley in England ; and our great northern towns, the most famous industrial centre in the world, with Manchester at the heart of it, and Leeds and Sheffield and Bradford and Halifax and Oldham and Huddersfield with their roaring mills and factories, their colleges and galleries and schools.

Turning down to Staffordshire our flying traveller would see the spires of Lichfield, the pottery towns, Shakespeare's Warwickshire with the beautiful river he loved, the church where he lies, the cottage where he was born, the hall in which he saw his first play, and the school in which he learned to write. He would see Birmingham with its thousand trades sending things to the ends of the earth ; Coventry, the capital of the motor-car world, where the wheels never stop ; and Warwick Castle, started by Alfred's daughter with a little mound still standing, fortified by the Conqueror, and preserved through twenty generations as one of the noblest surviving houses in the world. His eye would fall on the ruins of Kenilworth, and on to London through Oxford with its towers of learning, through Reading with its marvellous treasure-house from Roman Silchester, by the Buckinghamshire home of John Hampden, and taking in Windsor, where Edward the Confessor lived before the Conqueror.

Nowhere in the world could a man flying in the boundless realms of space look down on a scene so moving to those who love freedom, so fraught with significance for all mankind, as on the fifty thousand square miles of England.   To us it is a little paradise with all the beauty Nature gave it, but how much history it has seen !   How much character it has built up that has woven itself into the life of the world !

Our flying man can go up with the lark and look down on it all, and well may we wonder what his thoughts will be as he sits up there.   He will see the life of our people as it is, and will think of all it has been.   He will see old shepherds standing on green hills with sheep-dogs looking up into their eyes ; a doctor riding over a moor all purple and gold to a whitewashed cottage where a mother rocks a child by a window ; postmen trudging up steep hills with their red bicycles ; spires of churches rising above elm-trees where the rooks have been building for hundreds of years ; cottages in gardens full of flowers and great houses with their stately terraces ; men and children clustering round the door of the blacksmith's forge ; the cobbler at his last in his leather apron, the tailor with his needle, and the baker at the bin ; thousands of men building houses, making cars, driving engines, erecting bridges ; great ships gliding away to sea with the flag of England hanging from their sterns ; cricket on the green, boating on the river, and tennis on the lawn ; the ceaseless traffic on the roads ; the great furnaces glowing with fire ; and the machinery that never stops.

And, thinking of all he sees, our flying man will remember what has happened here.   In his imagination he will see Alfred crowned at Winchester and the

Conqueror crowned there too. He will see centuries of struggle and war with the forest shrinking back from the field, but always with a little group left together—the church, the hall, the farm, the cottage, and the inn. He will see the towns grown up on the banks of the rivers, and great churches and towering monasteries, the passing of the Conqueror's men and the coming of the English kings, and the slow growing-up of the power of the people. He will see John Wycliffe preaching from the pulpit at Lutterworth, where those who hated his English Bible were to dig up his bones and throw them in the river ; and William Tyndale choosing exile and facing death that he might give the Bible to the English people.

He will see thousands of poor students crowding to the colleges of Oxford and Cambridge, and hear the peasants singing in the fields the words of the Bible in their own tongue. He will see Chaucer riding with the pilgrims to pray at the shrine of Thomas Becket, some of the pilgrims a little over-merry, but all of them kind and many of them gentle, and all speaking of the change that had come to England and wondering what other change lay ahead. He will see the glory of Elizabeth with Drake and Raleigh and Hawkins and Martin Frobisher sailing for distant lands ; Edmund Spenser reading his Faerie Queene to Sir Walter Raleigh, and Shakespeare walking to London ; the Armada sweeping like a fire before a gale off the English coast ; Francis Bacon writing ; Ben Jonson in the Mermaid Tavern ; barges passing under London Bridge with the towering shops along it. He will see the first coach brought from Holland as a gift for Queen Elizabeth, and the new fashion of travelling on wheels crowding the narrow streets of London, while the boatmen on the Thames march to Westminster with a petition against the ruin of their trade.

He will see the Mayflower go from Plymouth to seek a new world for men who would be free, John Hampden looking stern, John Milton dreaming, and Cromwell victorious at Naseby. He will see the Stuarts come and go—Charles Stuart's head falling in Whitehall on a snowy day, and then Oliver Cromwell's stuck on a pike in the wind and the rain for twenty-five years. He will see the Stuarts back, with bells ringing and flags flying and dancing everywhere, and every kind of evil surging towards King Charles's court. Yet he will see a poor tinker in Bedford prison writing The Pilgrim's Progress, and blind Milton dreaming of Paradise in his little Buckinghamshire garden, and, as the Stuarts go out, the Duke of Marlborough leading his armies to victories which astonish the world. Sir Isaac Newton is giving men new truths of the universe, and Christopher Wren is building St Paul's.

Our flying man sees the rise of the towns, and the coming of the German kings to England, and the refusal of the aristocracy to go to court with them, but going instead to their estates in the country and there becoming farmers on a mighty scale, so that from this time England has been famous in the world for her fine cattle. He sees the nation growing strong in the east and in the west, gathering under her protection both India and America, and standing in Europe against the tyranny of Napoleon. He sees Nelson dying on the Victory at Trafalgar, Wellington home triumphant after Waterloo, Napoleon on St Helena, and he thinks of one of our poets who, sailing past Trafalgar, cried out from his heart :

Nobly, nobly Cape Saint Vincent to the north-west died
  away ;
Sunset ran, one glorious blood-red, reeking into Cadiz
  Bay ;
Bluish 'mid the burning water, full in face Trafalgar
  lay ;
In the dimmest north-east distance dawned Gibraltar
  grand and grey ;
Here and here did England help me : how can I help
  England ? say.

So the vision passes as our flying man looks down.
The hundred years since then have been the greatest
years for all mankind, and for us they have been a
crowning triumph. We kept America safe by suggesting to her the Monroe Doctrine which has kept
her enemies away from the continent. We freed the
slaves and set liberty marching on. We lived through
the Victorian Era, the greatest single reign in history,
with votes for every house and education for all, with
railways, ships, and telegraphy, and the way made
easy for democracy.

The Great War threw its shadow over all, but we
held fast, and for four winters our country guarded
civilisation and held the fort for liberty. We kept
alive the faith of the weak and the strong. We kept
our name clean at a cost grievous to be borne. We
suffered humiliation and disaster, but we planted
hope in the hearts of millions of stricken people in
hunger, chains, and slavery. We raised our country
in those years to the very height of hope and faith
and power. We realised a strength of which we had
not dreamed. We tapped new wealth and power
lying unsuspected all about us. We found that we
could do gigantic things of which we had been afraid.

We made the great discovery that a nation loving peace over all could be transformed in a night to fight for peace with all the stern terror of war. To the ends of the earth we sent out our armies and fleets. They fought amid the ice and snow, flung their bridges across the rivers, and marched across the sands. They rose above the clouds and descended into the sea. They fought in marsh and jungle and on Alpine heights. Their energies swept through every continent. Their dauntless spirit stirred the world.

We raised eight million men and a thousand pounds for every man. We maintained in food and fighting power the greatest armies ever raised, separated by thousands of miles of land and sea. We handled fifty million separate things every week in our munition shops, and sent out ten thousand consignments every working day. We transported by sea a multitude of thirteen million men, two million horses and mules, seven hundred thousand vehicles, and more than fifty million tons of supplies. We laid down hundreds of thousands of miles of railways. We had six hundred steamers always carrying troops, seven hundred on the waterways of France, and thirteen hundred vessels travelling up the Tigris every day. We built millions of tons of new ships and repaired forty thousand vessels of war. We defended a coastline of nearly eight thousand miles.

No book could tell of all the things our country did in those four years, but one thing all men know— that the spirit of liberty, when the enemy came, raised up its defenders to the ends of the earth, so that those who loved peace were more than a match for all those who loved war.

It was a Frenchman who said that it consoled him for a thousand crimes to look across the sea at this little island in its proud majesty, calm amid all the deliriums of mankind, and it was this same Frenchman, Victor Hugo, who wrote :

> *I love this little island lone and wild,*
> *Where England, Freedom's child,*
> *Neath its old flag doth Right maintain.*

So others think. As for us, perhaps we may like best those simple words of Charles Mackay :

> *There's a land, a dear land, where the rights of the free,*
> *Though firm as the earth, are as wide as the sea ;*
> *Where the primroses bloom, and the nightingales sing,*
> *And the honest poor man is as good as a king.*

THE EMPIRE

ON an October morning in the dawn of last century an Englishman woke and said to those about him, "Now, gentlemen, let us do something today that the world will talk about hereafter." He was Admiral Collingwood, and he kept his word, for he finished the Battle of Trafalgar.

Not once nor twice but many times in our fair Island's story men have done something that the world would talk about hereafter. We cannot imagine the time when the world will cease to talk of the British Empire. There has been no other Empire like it. Our flag flies over regions Caesar never knew. Long before the world talked of a League of Nations the British Empire had made one of its own. It is unique in history for its size, its variety, the multitude of its people, the extraordinary number of races to which they belong, the hundreds of languages they speak, their strange beliefs and religious faiths, and their varying degrees of civilisation. They inhabit every continent and hundreds of islands. They live in jungles, in wide open spaces, on the edge of the desert, on remote and almost inaccessible islands, in barbarous regions, in wild places where wolves come creeping round by night, sometimes fifty miles from neighbours, and in the greatest cities in the world.

All these have come together to find peace under the British Crown, and it is two or three lifetimes only that have seen the miracle. We have had Empires before and lost them (we lost one, as Germany lost hers, by a Treaty of Versailles), but never was an Empire like this, held by freedom and not by conquest, bound by an invisible chain stronger than the steel of a Dictator's sword.

What a story it has been, this building-up of the King's Dominions overseas since the days when Sir Walter Raleigh sat dreaming, his heart breaking over his Virginia. He would still see it an English land, he said, and he dreamed that the power of this Island would go out into the world and spread liberty and fine things everywhere. Has it not come true?

We have carried the blessings of civilisation to every continent. We have borne the heat and burden of the day to scatter freedom like the mustard seed that covers the earth. We have a Dominion which rules over more of America than the United States. We have a matchless Empire in Asia. We have a whole continent to call our own in the Southern Seas. We have lit a lamp in Darkest Africa that shines from end to end and can never be put out.

It is hard for an Englishman to look at the map of the world and not be moved. It is more than a map to him. It is something intimate, for everywhere his countrymen have fought and suffered and died, have swept away despotism, barbarism, and disease, made habitable the desert and the crooked ways straight, lit up dark places, cleared the jungle, and shattered the citadels of ignorance. The glory and the dream, the pathos and the tragedy, are all on the map of the world for us. Though our Island should be drowned again, the names of the men who went out from it, the things they dreamed of and the things they did, would live on in the deathless story of the world. Let us take just one of them, whose life is like an epitome of this Empire that covers one-quarter of the earth.

This great adventure of the British Empire began as an idea in the mind of Walter Raleigh. As Alfred dreamed of an English nation set in these narrow seas, Raleigh dreamed of an Empire beyond the raging main.

He was born in a farmhouse down in Devon, where we may see the kitchen he sat in, the windows he looked through, the very door he opened. The Reformation had burst the prison walls of thought ; the minds of men were opening out and they dared to speak. And there were things to speak about, for a beggarman from the streets of Madrid had found another world and America was drawing ships into it like a magnet.

Raleigh found his way to court. He dreamed like a poet and lived like a lord in his palace by the Thames. He walked through the streets wearing a hatband of pearls, and though he owned great lands he worked as hard as any man. He obtained from Queen Elizabeth a charter to organise a fleet and go to sea, and to do what had not been done before—to provide for the occupation of the country he discovered, so that men should be able to go there and colonise new corners of the world. It happened that Queen Elizabeth would not let Raleigh go, so that his expedition sailed without him, to his great grief, while he stayed at home to entertain the Queen. He told her she should have a better Indies than the King of Spain.

THE KING AND HIS FAMILY

His expedition left a hundred people in Virginia, and it was like a Golden Age to them until they were betrayed by the Red Indians, when food ran short and they were menaced by starvation. Suddenly Francis Drake appeared and gave them passage home, and they had hardly left when Sir Richard Grenville called with ships and stores. Not finding the people there, he left fifteen volunteers as an outpost on Roanoke Island, the only foot of territory then held secure for England. Raleigh sent out a new expedition to these men but could not find them, and we may think of this lonely group of Englishmen on the edge of an unknown world as the first martyrs of the Empire.

Tragedy on tragedy befell his expeditions, but there was no despair in Raleigh's heart. The American coast had been explored for 250 miles and he had found friendly peoples, and potatoes, and tobacco, and mahogany. Five expeditions to Virginia he sent out. One of them was under the famous John Smith whose life was saved by Pocahontas, the Red Indian princess who befriended Raleigh's people, married an Englishman, came to England, went to see a Shakespeare play, and was buried by the Thames. In charge of another expedition was Captain John White who brought home the sad news of the lost men of Roanoke, but who left behind him in Virginia over a hundred men, women, and children. One of the women was his daughter, who became the mother of Virginia Dare, the first child born in the British Empire oversea.

Virginia Dare! How great a name, and how true! It is pathetic to see how true was the instinct of Raleigh in the first great dream of his life. He had another, the breaking of the despotic power of Spain which threatened more and more to overwhelm these islands. It was this that brought him to his doom, for Queen Elizabeth died and the Stuarts came to the throne, and James the First came down from Scotland hating this great Englishman. He betrayed him to Philip of Spain and handed him over to the mercy of the Spanish ambassador. For years James kept him in the Tower, a captive in a cage, where the King's son, the young Prince of Wales, would come to talk to him, and would say, " Only my father would keep such a bird in a cage." When he had been in the Tower ten years, and was 62, he started to write a History of the World ; it is thought he may have written it for the young prince who loved him. Cromwell esteemed it as second to the Bible. Charles Kingsley called it the most God-fearing History ever known.

One day Raleigh woke up to find himself free to go out on a new expedition to seek a mine. He came out of the Tower and walked through the streets of London for the first time in ten years. We can imagine the familiar figure making his way through the streets by the Thames, startling little groups of people as he passed, turning into Adelphi, the scene of his great days, past Charing Cross, down Whitehall and on to Westminster, where he would turn into the solemn twilight of the Abbey to live again through memory by the tomb of Queen Elizabeth. But his doom was hastening on. The news that Raleigh was fitting out his ships again caused a stir in Madrid, the Spanish ambassador protested to the King, and in the end the last of this great company of Elizabeth's immortals was handed over to the mercy of Spain by the King himself, who let Raleigh go and behind his back gave the ambassador all his secret plans, and the promise that if Raleigh offended Spain King James himself would hand him over to be hanged in Madrid. Alas for the breaking hearts of men, the expedition failed, his own son perished, and Raleigh came home to be arrested in the name of Spain. They took him down to Old Palace Yard, and outside the walls of the Abbey his head fell to the ground. " I have a long journey to take, and must bid the company farewell," he said.

Victory and defeat, hope and tragedy, sunshine and cloud—it is the way of life and it has been the way of empires. Yet for centuries it was the dream of every spirited boy to go to sea and seek his fortune. Many never found it ; many never came back. The bones of thousands of them rest far from their English homeland, but where they lie is something for ever England. Not their dust alone was sown there, but the spirit of that English mother who sent them. Heart and body and mind and soul, England lives in the great Dominions oversea, springing from the seed the pioneers sowed with their lives.

There was that stout Devon man who sounded his drum in all the Seven Seas, Francis Drake with his Golden Hind. There was Sir Humphrey Gilbert who proclaimed Newfoundland the land of Queen Elizabeth. There was Sir Hugh Willoughby who tried to find the nearest way to India and perished with all his men in the Arctic, frozen as they sat in their cabins. There was old Martin Frobisher seeking his way through the North-West Passage, bringing home old stones he thought were gold, and breaking his heart to find they were only stones.

There was brave Henry Hudson of Hudson Bay ;
no man knows where in England he was born, and
none where he lies, but we know that he knelt with
his little son John to receive communion in a church
in Bishopsgate before he went to Greenland, and
sailed into the great bay that bears his name.
There were a dozen of them, and food ran short, his
crew rebelled, and they cast him adrift in an open
boat to pass out of history with his boy.   There was
that strange man William Dampier, who faced
astounding perils at sea, lived for weeks on goats and
turtles, and came home a broken man.   There were
the men who blazed the Canadian trail—Samuel
Hearne, who sought the Coppermine River and
followed it to the Arctic, and Alexander Mackenzie
who pushed on from Lake Athabasca to Mackenzie
River and to the Great Divide of the Rocky Mountains.   There was James Bruce, who began the
great epic of the unveiling of Darkest Africa by his
journey to the Blue Nile, and the men who traced
the African rivers, mapped the lakes, trod the forest,
and crossed the swamps : Mungo Park, Burton and
Speke, Samuel Baker, and David Livingstone.   And
there was Joseph Thomson, who found the great
Rift Valley and was the first white man to gaze on
Kilimanjaro lifting its head to the clouds above the
fruitful lands of Kenya.

There was our great and matchless Captain Cook,
who went out from his Yorkshire cottage and gave
a continent to the flag ; he put on the map the
names of Tahiti, the Society Islands, New Zealand,
and Australia.   He was the first known white man
to see the turquoise waters of the Coral Sea, but the
great thing he did for all mankind was to make life
at sea healthy for men everywhere.   Every boy

should raise his hat to his statue when he sees it, for by this great discovery he made our Empire possible.

The men who explored these vast possessions in Oceania were all of the spirit of Captain Cook. There were Bass and Flinders, who explored the east coast of Australia in their little cockleshell Tom Thumb. There were Blaxland and Oxley, who crossed the dense forests of the Blue Mountains. There was Charles Sturt, who found the River Darling, and Edward John Eyre, whose dramatic journeys in the desert are terrible reading, and Sir George Grey, who explored and developed the Promised Land which now teems with apples and wheat. And who can forget the bitter tale of Burke and Wills, who died in trying to cross the Australian Continent? They perished of starvation, leaving their story behind them.

How many Empires have we had? Canute won an Empire in Scandinavia, our early kings won one in France, and we had in our keeping the vast territory that is now the United States. All three are gone, and in their place has been built up the empire that we know, 150 years old or so, held firm without a conqueror's sword. The names of its founders and heroes and the shapers of its destiny ring in our history: Clive of Plassey, Wolfe of Quebec, Cecil Rhodes of Africa, Nelson and Wellington and Pitt, and the long line of statesmen who have built up scattered territories into great Dominions, who have united South Africa, federated Canada, and joined the States of Australia into a Continental Commonwealth. What harvests our Empire builders have prepared for us! What riches they opened up for their vast posterity! They sowed wheat East

and West, in South Africa and in India.   They set
out apple orchards in Australia and New Zealand,
in Canada and Tasmania.   Their sheep flourished on
the wide plains of Australia and in New Zealand's
green meadows.   Their cattle are everywhere ; even
in Nigeria and West Africa the traveller finds them.
Wheat and wool, meat and fruit, butter and cheese,
come back to the Island all the year round in a
thousand ships for every ship the heroes had to sail in.

The blessings they scattered on the waters to
return to us after many days grew out of the spirit
of the Island which has gone far out into the world.
Every Englishman loves his garden, and wherever
our heroes sailed and settled they tilled the land that
it should give them its fruits in due season.   In this
vast Empire, where always somewhere it is summer,
and where seed-time in one place is harvest-time in
another, the sun never sets and the supply never
ceases.   At every hour of the day a ship is nearing
home, bringing the fruits of the earth from some of
our great Dominions.

For hundreds of years the Island was pouring itself
into the Empire.   It gave the Empire its life and
strength, its men and its dreams, and today the
Empire is paying it back.   It will pay us back
a thousandfold if we will avail ourselves of its
miraculous wealth.   It can pour into our lap the
riches of the earth.   It can give us all we need to
eat and to wear.   There is never a week, never a
day, when something good is not on the way to us
from some corner of the Empire.

So illimitable are the dreams of this Empire that
one of our Prime Ministers predicted long ago that

the day would come when its capital would remove to Ottawa. It seems impossible to be extravagant in what we say of Canada, with its millions of square miles stretching from the Atlantic to the Pacific Ocean, with its twelve rich provinces fraught with destiny for its ten million people. Two of its provinces alone could maintain the population of the United States. It has great cities like Winnipeg, Toronto, Quebec, and Montreal. It has a chain of lakes with a water surface about as big as the British Isles. It has immense river systems, marvellous forests, and boundless prairies. It has unrivalled natural waterways, amazing mineral wealth, rich goldfields, and valuable fisheries. It has railways crossing the Continent from which the traveller looks out on golden wheatlands, impressive glaciers, vast forests, great mountains, and at times descends into grim canyons.

It is one of the greatest examples the world has seen of the fact that nations can live together in peace without making war and without building up arms, for in this great Dominion is a boundary line thousands of miles long marked with nothing but a few sticks and maintained without a single rifle or a single sentry. The peoples on each side of it have fought each other in their time, but have found it possible to live as neighbours for a hundred years. Even more remarkable, perhaps, is the fact that in this great Dominion French and English have lived at peace together longer still. The great province of Quebec is mostly French but follows its own ways, speaking its own language: French and Roman Catholic, here in loyalty they live in millions side by side with English Protestants, loyal to one flag, obedient to one governor, ruled by one councillor, governed by one code of laws. It is a noble and dramatic lesson for the world.

And so it is in South Africa, with two great races living side by side, sharing a country rich beyond all counting, with a future beyond all dreams.

Perhaps it is the future of Australia that sets men thinking deeply. There is no stranger story in the world than the story of its biggest Island or its smallest Continent. It was the last continent to be found and it was saved for the flag by a lucky chance, for a Yorkshireman arrived to claim it a day before a Frenchman. La Perouse found Captain Cook in possession and sailed away never to be heard of more. No man knows what fate befell this man who just missed presenting his country with a continent. The vast country so dramatically lost to France covers about 3,000,000 square miles, with a coastline 12,000 miles long. Round it is a fertile fringe, but the heart of it is a sandy and stony desert with saltwater lakes and grasslands here and there. It has ranges of alps which for years defied explorers but are now crossed by railways ; between the ranges are yawning chasms and deep gorges and fearful precipices. It has plants and animals like no others in the world, as if Nature had turned back and tried again. It has forests in which beeches grow a hundred feet before the branches come, and eucalyptus trees growing higher than St Paul's. In Queensland we may walk down avenues of orchids, past beds of arum lilies, between dark walls of myrtle, in forests still in their original magnificence.

It is incredible but true that we did not want this wondrous continent. We had no use for it when Captain Cook set up the flag there, just in time to make it ours, but twenty years after that we turned it into a convict prison, landing a shipload of convicts who for thirty years had the continent to themselves. We are a little wiser now, for Australia has great cities like Sydney and Melbourne and Adelaide and Brisbane and Perth ; she has federated her six States and spent more pounds than she has people on a new capital for it. She has 30,000 miles of railways and 150,000 miles of telegraph lines, and she has over a hundred million sheep with fifty million cattle and horses and pigs.

Australia is the only continent that has ever been ruled under one flag, a fact which carries with it dazzling opportunities. Alas, she has few people, for if this vast continent were divided equally among its people, every man, woman, and child in Australia would have two square miles. It is this that is so anxious a problem in a world with nations yearning for room to live.

Australia has still a little host of Blackfellows, her original inhabitants. They roam about the interior in tribes, little better (but let us hope little worse) for contact now and then with the civilisation that comes to their borders.

Not so is it with New Zealand, the Island Dominion a thousand miles away, where the Maoris, the original inhabitants, have risen to take their share in government, proud of their past and hopeful of their future. It is a long time since the first Governor of New South Wales declared that if the convicts misbehaved themselves he would give them to the natives of New Zealand to eat !

Today New Zealand is like another England across the world. No people in the Empire are more devoted to the Home Country. No other people buy so much from us at home. A marvellous little country about the size of its Motherland, it has alps with fine glaciers, scenery like Switzerland, and a coast deeply cut by magnificent fiords giving access to lofty mountains. It has remarkable regions with active and dead volcanoes, and with geysers and hot lakes. The two islands have every variety of scenery, and their contented people, with as peaceful a history as any people in the world, are outnumbered twenty times by their horses and cattle and sheep.

But what are we to say of India ? If the British Empire is the greatest political achievement in history, the Government of India is the greatest achievement in the Empire.

There is no spectacle on earth that can compare with the astonishing sight of the little host of men sent out from these islands to hold together this mighty multitude.

To talk with all these people a man must know two hundred languages. To understand their history he must go back as far as Solomon. To realise the real problem of India he must remember that little girls were thrown to the crocodiles not so very long ago, and that widows were burned alive when their husbands died. He must remember, too, a very terrible thing, that India has within her borders a mass of human beings loathed and hated by their countrymen, so that even their shadow falling on another is held to be unclean. For these Untouchables the British flag is the only hope, and there are more of these unhappy folk in India than there are white people in all the British Empire.

For sixty million hopeless human creatures our flag is all the guarantee they have of any life worth while.

This astounding country, looking like a red triangle on the map of the world, is as big as Europe without Russia. Its greatest length and its greatest breadth are each about 1900 miles. It is separated from the main continent of Asia by the Himalayas, the most stupendous mountain system in the world, with Everest as its crowning peak. From the beginning of recorded history down to the opening of the modern period this mountain barrier separated India from the main stream of the world's life, although it did not protect the Indian people from invasion and conquest. Nearly every great marauder of the East, tempted by stories of Indian treasure, has crossed the mountain-passes and descended to ravage the cities of the plain.

India contains within itself an almost unlimited variety of climate, scenery, vegetation, animals, and peoples. Its northern regions run far up into the Temperate Zone ; the southern part of the peninsula lies within the Tropics. The wide plains, where the important cities are, endure the most terrific heat during many months of the year. The hills and valleys provide some of the most romantic landscapes and some of the most delightful health resorts in the world. The superbly beautiful country of Kashmir is unexcelled among the playgrounds of men. Fruits of every clime grow abundantly. The land includes every variety of soil, from the fertile fields which yield three crops a year to stretches of arid desert where nothing will grow. It is a land of mighty rivers, renowned in history and reverenced as the bringers of life to the people. They nourish hundreds of cities and thousands of villages ; they are the scene of an unceasing and most picturesque activity, and for thousands of years they have carried an immense volume of trade.

The people of this vast country number about 350 millions. They are three in four of the whole population of the Empire and about one in six of the population of the world. They cover almost the entire range of civilisation from the savage to the most refined. They speak 220 languages, and a strange web of religious beliefs and practices runs through the whole country. The chief religion is Hinduism with its terrible system of Caste. Caste divides the people into hundreds of groups, and caste rules govern everything in the lives of Hindu men and women, eating and drinking, births and marriages and deaths—everything. To break the rules of caste means to become an outcaste ; it means death in life. The Untouchables are a direct result of the caste system.

For ages the life of India has changed little, and in vast parts of the country Macaulay's pictures of India, describing the days when Warren Hastings was Governor-General, would be true today. This is how Macaulay described one scene at Benares :

The traveller could hardly make his way through the press of holy mendicants and not less holy bulls.

The broad and stately flights of steps which descended from these swarming haunts were worn every day by the footsteps of an innumerable multitude of worshippers. The schools and temples drew crowds of pious Hindus from every province where the Brahminical faith was known.

Hundreds of devotees came hither every month to die, for it

*was believed that a peculiarly happy fate awaited the man who
should pass from the sacred city into the sacred river.*

This vast slow-moving mass of people was invaded
by Mohammedan conquerors over 400 years ago,
when the Mogul emperors established themselves
in power and shaped the system of administration
when the British began to take over in the 18th
century. The Moguls built the splendid cities which
travellers from the West admire for their magnificent design, and for the mosques and palaces that
are among the most perfect buildings in the world.

There is one great difference between the British
and all the earlier invaders of India. The earlier
invaders entered as military conquerors ; our people
entered as traders, about the time when Queen
Elizabeth was passing from the scene.

Their coming was made possible by that wonderful
feat which marks off the Middle Ages from the
modern period, the beginning of ocean navigation.
The East India Company, founded at the dawn of
the 17th century, was simply a company of London
merchants. They had no dreams of an empire in
the East. What they wanted was trade, but in the
middle of the 18th century the outlook was changed.
England and France were contending for world
empire in Canada and in India. It happened that
in the East India Company were two clerks who
had great dreams ; not traders were they, but empire
builders, and it was their genius and energy that
decided the destiny of India. They were Robert
Clive and Warren Hastings.

The Mogul Empire was in ruins, the Indian princes
were in perpetual conflict, and the East India Company grew ever more powerful until it ruled one-

third of India and had its own fleet and army; it acted like a sovereign power. Robert Clive on the battlefield (he won his famous victory at Plassey with 3200 against 50,000 men) made British power secure, and Warren Hastings as Governor-General consolidated the new Empire, until in the middle of last century it was shaken to its base by the mutiny of the Bengal Army. After that the powers of the Company were transferred to the Crown and the Queen of England became Empress of India.

It is not all India that is British, for the ruling princes retain their powers and privileges and govern their own States. These States (*of which there are over five hundred*) cover the immense area of 700,000 square miles, and two of them are as big as Great Britain ; two more as big as Scotland, and one as big as Wales. All these princes, most of whom have immense wealth, have a personal link with the British Crown, and have the right of access to the King, and all receive the protection of the flag. They receive the benefit of a system of British rule unique in the history of empires. It has given two generations of peace to India, with the one exception of the Mutiny. It is a miracle of order and skill. Our great India Services, with their many departments dealing with education, health, police, forests, and taxation, and the great network of other duties carried on by Indians themselves, are unrivalled in the world. The actual Civil Service is staffed by Indians and Britons alike, all entering by the door of open competition in England. These men rise to be magistrates, district judges, and commissioners, carrying on the work laid down by Warren Hastings, and they are never more in number than 1200. They labour during the greater part of

the year in the heat of the cities and the villages
of the plains, though the heads of the Government
and the public departments change their address
every year and go up to the hills when the great
heat comes. This terrific heat, which is too great
for white folk, lasts from April till October, and it is
a remarkable flitting that then takes place. The
Government of India spends the winter at Delhi and
the hot season at Simla, high up among the
mountains of the Punjab—the most elaborate and
most picturesque hill metropolis in the world. The
Bombay Government migrates to Poona ; the
Madras Government to Ootacamund, a delightful
place in the Nilgiri Hills ; the Bengal Government
to Darjeeling, 7000 feet above the plain, with the
marvellous range of Kinchinjunga full in view across
the mighty Himalayan valleys.

This Government, thus briefly described, is the
basis and the assurance of the wonderful structure
of modern India ; the guarantee of security for the
great systems of roads, railways, and irrigation
canals ; for the commerce and public services of
cities like Bombay, Calcutta, and Madras, Delhi and
Allahabad, Lahore, and Lucknow ; for the extraordinary industrial development of the cotton mills
of Bombay and Nagpur, the woollen mills of
Cawnpore, the jute and tea of Bengal and Assam,
the iron and steel so rapidly growing that since the
war India has taken its place among the great metal-
manufacturing countries ; for the irrigated wheat
colonies of the North, by virtue of which India now
stands among the foremost grain-producing countries
of the world ; for the mining enterprises and the
great banking, insurance, and shipping houses. In
all these the world has confidence because the

British Government is there. It need not be less confident, we may hope, because the future of a self-governing India looms before us.

It would be like an ever-changing kinematograph to run round the British Empire and see all its quaint and odd places, all the great sights of its big Dominions, and the scenery in its colonies and protectorates and dependencies. We should find such places as Inaccessible Island, a lofty mass of rock two miles long inhabited by penguins ; or Nightingale Island in charge of seals and sea-elephants. We should come to the familiar but little-visited Tristan da Cunha, with its lonely family of about a hundred folk who see one or two ships in a year and have no other communication with the world. We should come to volcanic islands now producing coconuts and sugar-cane and cotton and rice—there are two hundred volcanic islands in the Fiji group alone. We should find on one of our islands (in Trinidad, only seven miles from the American mainland) a pitch lake of a hundred acres which provides the surface for miles of London's streets ; 50,000 tons of asphalt are taken from it in one year. We should find the famous island of Jamaica, discovered by Columbus in one century, settled by the Spaniards in the next, taken over by England in the next. It has a million loyal people living in three counties called Surrey, Middlesex, and Cornwall, and it has Blue Mountains from which seventy streams run down to the sea a mile and a half below the peaks. We should find ourselves in the lovely island of Ceylon at the foot of India, which gives the world one in every six of its cups of tea, and a vast number of its lead pencils. We should find islands such as Bermuda, which has neither

streams nor natural wells, but depends for water
on storing its rainfall in tanks and artificial wells.
It has done this so ingeniously that it has become
one of America's health resorts. We should find
vast native kingdoms of Africa, such as Basutoland,
Bechuanaland, and Swaziland, with huge populations
of black folk, hundreds of thousands of cattle, and
only a small group of white people. We should
come to great countries like Uganda, where native
kings are encouraged to rule their own people
and to develop their country by growing cotton ;
like Nigeria, with twenty million people, rich
minerals, fertile soil, fine forests, good ports, and
a thousand miles of railways ; like Kenya, four
times as big as England, with an ideal climate,
three million people, and the second biggest fresh-
water lake in the world humming with steamers.
We should come upon the marvellous territory of
the Soudan, with over a million square miles through
whose swamps and forests the Nile and its tributaries
carry wealth to Egypt. It has been a battlefield
in living memory and has now great cornfields, vast
areas of it having been irrigated so that it sends
cotton out to the world and supplies all the meat
that Egypt needs.

We should come upon some of the most remarkable
natural spectacles in the world and some of the most
impressive places. We should see Niagara rushing
on and falls of water greater still ; we should see the
Zambesi, a thousand yards wide, leaping suddenly
down 400 feet into a winding gorge, with a forest
eternally watered by the spray, and smaller falls
close by whose spray is like a rainbow in the sun.
In Uganda we should see the Ripon Falls where the
Victoria Nyanza gushes forth in a triple cascade of

rare beauty to give birth to the Nile.   We should see
Kalambo Falls, dividing Rhodesia and Tanganyika,
dropping 1700 feet over a precipice into a tropical
forest.   We should see the great Falls on Hamilton
River in Labrador dropping 800 feet and making one
of the grandest sights in North America.   We
should see the Great Rift Valley, the biggest crack
in the world, running down Africa for 2500 miles,
from the valley of the Jordan in Palestine to the
Lake Nyasa found by Livingstone.   We should see
Kilimanjaro with its head in clouds and mist 20,000
feet up, the roof of Africa, its volcanic crater filled
with ice and snow and big enough to hold all our
English cathedrals.   We should see the Kalahari
desert, the marvellous home of African races that
have perished elsewhere, with 300,000 square miles,
a network of river beds mostly dried up, and Lake
Ngami which is now filled up after being dry for a
hundred years.   In this great desert area, barred
by desert wastes, shifting sands, and impenetrable
thorn bush, is preserved all that is most interesting
in Africa's primitive life.   We should see the wonderful sanctuary of wild life and wild people in New
Guinea, the dead heart of Australia with its dis-
appearing lakes, the forests and jungle and deserted
cities of India, and the Great Barrier Reef sixty
miles from Australia, a spectacle unmatched in the
world, 1200 miles long with its coral builders glowing
in as many colours as Joseph's coat.

But among all the wonderful sights the Empire
traveller sees is none to compare with the Empire
in itself.   It is the miracle of the modern world,
unmatched in history.   It is the noblest spectacle
ever presented to mankind of the lion lying down
with the lamb.   It has been built up in strange,

mysterious ways, almost against our will, and it is
hardly more than sixty years since an English
Prime Minister declared that it was a millstone
round our neck. It has wealth beyond our dreams
and possibilities beyond imagining, yet we have sent
out to it only a small percentage of our crowded
island, and the population of white people in all the
British dominions overseas is not equal to three
Londons. And yet it has the greatest group of
self-governing communities upon the earth.

Never have so many loyal people been brought
together under one flag. No man has ever doubted
the passionate loyalty of the New Zealander, the
affectionate longing of the Australian to see the
Homeland, the pride of Canada in its high imperial
place, the unshakable spirit of loyalty that has
triumphed over all the troubles of South Africa.

Everywhere the masses of the people of our far-
flung realms are faithful to the flag which shelters
them. They are contented with their ways of government. They have no ill-will against any nation
in the world. They wish to see in every land the
same well-ordered way of life that they enjoy.
Gladly would they lay down arms and share their
quiet peace with all mankind.

One test there is of the success or failure of a
nation : how does its credit stand ? The measure
of the security of life in any land is the confidence of
the world in it. In the days when confidence has
almost broken down, there is everywhere a boundless
faith in the King's Dominions. Their debts count
up to ten thousand million pounds, yet there is not
a country in the world that would hesitate to lend
them more.

THE FLAG

NO prouder flag flies in the wind than ours. It is true that the sun never sets on it, for this gay strip of red, white, and blue follows the sun wherever he goes.

The British flag for a thousand years has braved the battle and the breeze, yet it is not for battles that we love it : it is the best flag in the world for us because it stands for what we love best, for all the things we mean when we think of England and the English-speaking people.

It is the friendliest flag the world has ever known, for no man fears it. Wherever it is seen the slave knows he is free, the oppressed can come for help, the righteous cause can call for sympathy.

It is three flags in one, and it is arranged ingeniously so that all three have equal shares. It is thrilling to remember that the three flags stand for a Slave, a Soldier, and an Apostle.

The slave was carried to Ireland at the beginning of the fifth century and lived there thirty years, founding schools and monasteries, and dying there a very old man, to be remembered as St Patrick. The soldier was our famous St George, who killed the dragon and saved the king's daughter, and gave up his life rather than deny his faith at the bidding of a Roman emperor. The Apostle was St Andrew, one of the first two disciples Jesus called, who gave up all and followed Him, and was crucified on a cross.

Pity, courage, faithfulness unto death—it is not unfitting that these three should meet on the flag of a nation that has freed the slaves, has fought the dragons, and has carried Christianity to the ends of the earth. It is the red cross of St George, the white cross of St Andrew, and the red cross of St Patrick that make up the Union Jack. We may think it rather a pity that the red dragon of Wales has not a corner on it, for it is the most ancient standard in the western world, brought to Britain by the Romans and carried into battle by Welsh warriors to oppose the white horse of the Saxons. The red dragon is missing because Wales was one with England before the flag of St. George was made, and the three flags became one by their union with Ireland and Scotland. The cross of St Andrew on its blue ground was the national flag of Scotland, and was added at the beginning of the seventeenth century, when the crowns of England and Scotland were united. The red cross of St Patrick on a white ground was added at the beginning of the nineteenth century at the time of the union with Ireland.

And now this flag flies at the crowning of King George, at the dawn of a new era for our race. It flies at its masthead in our days of gladness ; it flies half-mast in our hours of grief. It is the familiar and universal symbol of the British people. It flies over a quarter of the earth and on ships on every sea. It is the very breath of life to us, for if alien hands should tear it down the life we love is at an end.

This Island Home that guards our flag has made it what it is, red with the blood of heroes, blue with

the sea, white as the soul of justice.   For a thousand
years our Motherland has been building up her
power in the world, and she is not unworthy of the
glory of her hills and dales, of the beauty of her
fields and lanes, and of the rolling downs that sweep
majestically to the sea.   She is not unworthy of the
silver sea that guards her body like a wall, for she
has set her throne upon the sea and rules it with a
sceptre fair to all :   the sea that has kept her free she
has freely repaid in full.   She is not unworthy of the
heroes who have died for her, of the thousand years
of sacrifice and patient toil that have made these
islands thrill with pride throughout the centuries.

Before our yeomen cut their bows from the ancient
yews still standing at our churchyard gates, before
the acorns were dropped in the earth to grow into
oaks for our wooden ships, the spirit of freedom found
its home in England, and out into the world it has
gone, far and wide to the ends of the earth, so that
there is not a free land anywhere, nor a free mind
under the sun, that would not suffer if our flag
should fall.

No enemy has ever pulled it down.   It has waved
on the battlefield that has made men free ; it has
sheltered the homeless and the refugee, and the
victims of tyrants in many lands ; it has kindled the
fire of heroes who have marched to liberty against
great odds.   It has been the torch of hope that
nothing could put out.   It has been like a fire of
freedom sweeping through the ages, or like a wind
blowing out of its path whatever hindered the
triumphant marching of the human race.

In all the strivings and longings of multitudes of
men it has been on the side of everlasting Right.   In

all the long story of the rise of nations it has been
on the side of freedom and peace. In the coming
up of the world from barbarism to civilisation it has
been on the side of humanity. It has cleansed the
world from many a foul blot, and hurled down many
a blood-stained power. It has sown the seed of
happiness, not as in a garden or a little plot of earth,
but generously and widely in a boundless land, for
all mankind to reap.

We should guard it well, this flag in whose folds
we live ; for it is woven with the lives of men and
women. Our freedom has not fallen from the skies,
like some great blessing for the world direct from
Heaven. Slowly it has been built up and many a
tale of toil and sorrow our flag tells. Francis Drake
was wrapped in it when they dropped him in the sea
he loved so well. It was flying on the Royal George
when Kempenfelt went down with twice four hundred men. It was on the Titanic when it sank, the
greatest ship at sea on its maiden voyage, and on
the R101 when it burst into flames, our greatest air-
ship on its maiden voyage ; almost the only thing
saved from that bitter fire was the flag that fell from
the sky, and we may see it still in the little church
of Cardington. It was with Captain Scott in his tent
and with Gordon at Khartoum. It has covered all
our kings on their last ride. It flew on the walls of
Lucknow on that thrilling day when the hard-
pressed garrison caught the sound of the bagpipes
playing " The Campbells are Coming." It flew on
our ships in the storm that sent the Spanish Armada
to its doom. It flew at Scutari over the hospital in
which our dying soldiers kissed the shadow of
Florence Nightingale as she passed by. It flew for
all those million men who went away to France and

Palestine and Egypt and Gallipoli and never came home again. It has been through all our darkest and saddest days.

Wonderful sights our flag has looked down on from the days of Alfred till now. It saw the passing of the little Saxon world that Alfred knew and the coming of the Norman, the only conqueror it has ever seen. A long, slow journey it has been since then, from an England with no English language, with a foreign king, with an enslaved people, to the kingdom of the flag that stirs the world. It is worth while looking at the steps by which we came.

The Norman Conquest did for England what British rule has done for India ; it drew together the scattered factions in the realm and shaped them into a nation. It paved the way for the beginnings of ordered rule, so that a hundred years later an English king was able to create an instrument of government of which something has survived till now. The great barons had grown too strong, like little kings in their castles, with kingly power over the men who tilled their land and responded to the summons if the barons should call them to arms. Now the power of the barons was checked ; the rule of Parliament began. Trade, politics, and literature grew up, and with the rise of industry came the growth of towns.

A race that sticks to the land like a limpet, an historian has said, cannot be great, however happy it may be ; and the breaking away of the English people from the land was one of their great strides forward. The English mind was broadening ; the feudal rule of the castle and the narrowing power of the priest were broken, and at last came Queen

THE FLAG ON A KENT HILLTOP

Elizabeth and her Golden Age—so great at home
that a law was passed for every cottage to have four
acres of its own ; so great abroad that Drake sailed
round the world and broke the tyranny of Spain.

At home and abroad the great building-up went
on. In many a cottage were laid the foundations of
that boundless commerce which has made ours the
richest country in the world. The little house with
its four acres seems to us now, as we look back, a true
symbol of the future that was coming, for it was the
little centre of agriculture and industry in one,
embracing the twin pillars of our national prosperity.
While the labourer looked after the farm his mistress
was busy at her spinning-wheel and his master at
the loom. The produce was sold or consumed, and
the cloth was sent on a pack-horse to the fair.

While industry was thus springing up, the inven-
tor's brain was thinking out machines, statesmen
were making broader laws, and in the end, with
Scotland and Ireland to help her, England was great
enough to save Europe from Napoleon, and to win
the mastery of the seas. Now for a hundred years
the power of the nation has been slowly rising, until
today our British Isles have nearly fifty million loyal
people in them, and beyond these islands our flag
flies over the lives and homes of hundreds of millions
of the human race.

North and south and east and west it flies, over
wide untenanted spaces and crowded cities, over
lands emerging from barbarism and over ancient
civilisations, over every continent and hundreds of
races and tribes. Not a church nor a faith is there
which is not worshipped under the British flag ; not

a language among men which is not spoken somewhere in its shadow.

Across the hot sands of the Nile Valley, over the
broad veld of South Africa, through the spacious bush-
lands of Australia, by the rivers of New Zealand, in
the matchless territories of Canada and Newfoundland, above the rich cities of India, the sheltering flag
waves in the breeze as the sign of human freedom,
and wherever it waves it is loved and cherished as
we love and cherish the things that are all in all.

It carries through Time a message of goodwill to
all who are free, a message of hope to all who are in
chains.   It bears from age to age, as if it were the
very breath of it, the everlasting spirit of mankind.
It is the sign and token that liberty has not perished
from the earth.   It stands for what these islands have
stood for like a rock throughout the ages, the right
of Liberty and Truth to march wherever they will,
hand in hand unhindered.

Perhaps we should not allow ourselves to think too
highly of ourselves ; let us see what others think of
what we stand for in the world.   It was a great
Frenchman who said that in England, if a man had
as many enemies as hairs on his head, no harm would
come to him ; and it was a famous American, Ralph
Waldo Emerson, who stood before a great audience
in Manchester and paid this tribute to our race :

Is it not true that the wise ancients did not praise the
ship parting with flying colours from the port, but only that
brave sailer which came back with torn sheets and battered
sides, stripped of her banners, but having ridden out the
storm ?

So I feel in regard to this aged England, with the possessions, honours, and trophies, and also with the infirmities

of a thousand years gathering around her (irretrievably committed as she now is to many old customs which cannot be suddenly changed, pressed upon by the transitions of trade, and new and all incalculable modes, fabrics, arts, machines, and competing populations), I see her not dispirited, not weak, but well remembering that she has seen dark days before—indeed with a kind of instinct that she sees a little better in a cloudy day, and that in storm of battle and calamity she has a secret vigour and a pulse like a cannon.

I see her in old age, not decrepit but young, and still daring to believe in her power of endurance and expansion ; and, seeing this, I say, All hail ! mother of nations, mother of heroes.

It was a famous Spaniard, George Santayana, who, when asked what it is that governs the Englishman, answered that it is his inner atmosphere, the weather in his soul. The Englishman, said he, is instinctively no conqueror, no missionary, but prefers rather to be aloof from strangers ; and yet he will be friendly and hospitable, and, as for his adventures, they are all outside his inner life and change him so little that he is not afraid of them :

He carries his English weather in his heart wherever he goes, and it becomes a cool spot in the desert, and a steady and sane oracle among all the deliriums of mankind. Never since the heroic days of Greece has the world had such a sweet, just, boyish master. It will be a black day for the human race when scientific blackguards, conspirators, churls, and fanatics manage to supplant him.

It was a Swede, the famous Swedenborg, who paid us the very high compliment of saying that, as for the English nation, the best of them are in the centre of all Christians, because *they have in their inner being an intellectual light*.

Frenchman, American, Spaniard, and Swede—
we may accept them as international spectators
looking on, seeing the work and the character of
the English people. What is it that our flag has
done for all mankind ? It has opened the gates
of the world and has opened the door of the human
mind. When the despotic power of Spain was at
its height, when her ships drove other countries
from the sea and the Inquisition gripped the human
mind as in a vice, the ships that broke this cruel
power flew England's flag. It was little England
(little then indeed) that shattered the power which
sentenced every Protestant in Holland to be put
to death.

It was our flag that flew on the first ship captained
by one man around the world. In those days of
our Golden Age our ships swept into new ports like
stars streaming into new worlds. Our flag threw
open the gates which Spain had locked and barred,
and broke the desolating tyranny of her war against
the spread of thought. No more could Spain stop
men thinking by pressing the thumbscrew and the
rack ; no longer was it a crime to seek or speak the
truth. It is the glory of our flag that under it a
man may think and say the thing he will. Always
wherever the flag has flown England has been
willing for knowledge and power to spread throughout mankind.

She broke the power of Spain that the seas might
be free. She broke the power of Napoleon that
Europe might be free. She burdened her present
and mortgaged her future to stay the hand of the
destroyer on a continent in which she did not own
enough land to dig a grave. It has not mattered

to her where the need and the cry have been ; she
has responded if she could. It is the spirit of the
flag. It is the spirit of the plague-stricken village
which shut itself off from the world until the plague
consumed it ; the spirit of the men of the Birkenhead
who put the women and children in the boats and
went down into the sea saluting England ; the spirit
of Kate Barlass who bolted the door with her arm
against the enemy ; the spirit of Grace Darling
who plunged into the angry sea with her little boat
from her father's lighthouse ; the spirit of a countless
host of men and women and children who have died
for the flag.

What is it that they lived and died for ? What
is it that stirs the blood of a hero when he gives his
life to save the flag from stain ? It is something
in us all that has come to us from we know not
where, that has grown in us we know not how,
because it is the very soul of the land we love. It
is the invisible fountain from which a nation's
greatness springs.

It is the something that made Alfred love the
truth, that moved Sir Francis Drake to finish the
game before he drove back the Armada, that kept
alive the pride of Walter Raleigh in the traitor's
cell, that put in Shakespeare's hand the power the
world can never take away, that touched the mind
of Milton with the glow of Paradise, that lit the
fire in Cromwell's soul, that stirred the vision of
John Bunyan, that nerved John Hampden to resist
a lawless king. It is the something that moved the
men of Cromwell's army who never lost a fight,
that gave to England in her hour of need the three
stout hearts of Wellington and Nelson and Pitt,

that touched the heart of William Wilberforce and would not let him rest until the slaves were free. It is the something that language has not yet found words for, this spirit that our men are ever dying for, this spirit that our flag is ever flying for.

It flies for all those things that have built up, out of the warring peoples of Alfred's day, the great ruling race of the world. It flies for the spirit that runs through the woof and texture of the English-speaking race. It flies to keep alive the hope of men that the days of war and strife will pass and that nations will live together as good neighbours. It flies for the government of the people, for the people, by the people, and for the greatest good of the greatest number. It flies for liberty for all who are able to use it and will not abuse it, and for guiding all others along the road that leads to it.

It flies (whatever the difficulties of these days may be) for the Open Door, a fair field and equal rights for all nations.

It flies for the gospel that the labourer is worthy of his hire, and that men shall not be slaves.

It flies for humanity in all things, for Justice and Mercy, for the stopping of cruelty, for kindness to animals, for the love of little children.

It flies for the honour of the spoken and written word throughout the world.

It flies for throwing open as wide as can be the field of human knowledge.

It flies for spreading as wide as can be the field of human happiness.

It flies for letting Truth be free as life itself.

It flies for the toleration of every man's opinion.

It flies for the unselfish pursuit of the good of all mankind.

It flies for the peace of all the world, which no nation ever longed for more.

All this is woven in the flag that flies at the four quarters of the globe, on every sea and on every wind. From these islands to the remotest corners of the earth this spirit has gone out, and nothing has been able to destroy it. It has gone into strange lands, it has been alone in the wilderness ; it has been in the Valley of the Shadow of Death ; but it has found its way and won. Its patience, somebody has said, is as long as a summer's day, but its arm is as long as a winter's night.

Driven from the Old World, it built up the New. The spirit that built up our Island Home cemented the foundations of America. It found Australia and established liberty firmly there. It is making India united and free. It has made South Africa happy and contented. It has brought Egypt out of barbarism and bondage. It is not as quick as lightning, but it is slow and sure. It sets out and gets there, muddling through at times but winning at last. It has the patience that knows that the dream must come true. It endures to the end. It cares not who dies if Freedom lives.

It has given to the world a glory that will not fade away. There is a glory of the sun, and a glory of the moon, and there is the glory of the flag. Greece and Rome have passed away, but the work of the flag endures.

It is not for nothing that the sun never sets on this banner of our ancient land.   Out of the historic past it flies, the assurance to mankind that Freedom lives.   In its sheltering folds lives one quarter of this troubled world, calm amid storms, free from all terrors, walking unafraid.